FIELD NOTES FOR THE WILDERNESS

Practices for an Evolving Faith

SARAH BESSEY

T0338819

First published in the United States of America in 2024 by Convergent Books, an imprint of Random House, a division of Penguin Random House LLC, New York

First published in Great Britain in 2024

SPCK
SPCK Group, The Record Hall, 16-16A Baldwins Gardens, London, EC1N 7RJ

www.spck.org.uk

This edition published by arrangement with Convergent Books, an imprint of Random House, a division of Penguin Random House LLC, New York

Book design by Diane Hobbing

Scripture quotations marked (MSG) are taken from *The Message,* copyright © 1993, 2002, 2018 by Eugene H. Peterson. Used by permission of NavPress. All rights reserved. Represented by Tyndale House Publishers. Scripture quotations marked (NIV) are taken from the Holy Bible, New International Version®, NIV®. Copyright © 1973, 1978, 1984, 2011 by Biblica Inc.™ Used by permission of Zondervan. All rights reserved worldwide. (www.zondervan.com). The "NIV" and "New International Version" are trademarks registered in the United States Patent and Trademark Office by Biblica Inc.™ Scripture quotations marked (NLT) are taken from the Holy Bible, New Living Translation, copyright © 1996, 2004, 2015 by Tyndale House Foundation. Used by permission of Tyndale House Publishers, Carol Stream, Illinois 60188. All rights reserved. Scripture quotations marked (NRSV) are taken from the NRSV Cultural Backgrounds Study Bible, copyright © 2019 by Zondervan. All rights reserved worldwide. (www.zondervan.com). Scripture quotations marked (FNV) are taken from *First Nations Version,* copyright ©2021 by Rain Ministries Inc. Used by permission of InterVarsity Press, Downers Grove, IL. All rights reserved.

Portions of the story about finding water in Arizona in Chapter 1 appeared in a different version in *Field Notes* newsletter on May 11, 2022. A section of the roll call in Chapter 1 appeared in an Evolving Faith sermon on October 14, 2022, and the invitations of Jesus in another Evolving Faith sermon on October 4, 2019. Portions of the story about losing prayer in Bonn in Chapter 2 appeared in a different version in *Field Notes* newsletter on May 5, 2021. A small portion of the silt-settling story in Chapter 3 appeared in a different version in *Field Notes* newsletter on October 26, 2020. Portions of the story about listening to Rich Mullins in Chapter 4 appeared in a different format in *Field Notes* newsletter on September 19, 2019. Portions of the Emmaus story in Chapter 5 appeared in an earlier form in an Evolving Faith sermon on October 2, 2020. Portions of the story with the midwife in Chapter 6 appeared in an earlier version on Sarah Bessey's blog on September 23, 2015. Portions of the story of the little girls in the dark in Chapter 7 appeared in a different version in *Field Notes* newsletter on February 22, 2022. A portion of the story in the Metropolitan Museum of Art in Chapter 7 appeared on Sarah Bessey's blog on October 6, 2017. A portion of the story at the lake with the kids in Chapter 10 appeared in a previous version in *Field Notes* newsletter on January 15, 2020. A small portion of the definition of Church in Chapter 11 appeared in a different version in *Field Notes* newsletter on October 25, 2021. A portion of the story on learning the truth about residential schools in Chapter 12 appeared in a different version on Sarah Bessey's blog on April 5, 2018. A portion of the story on moving in Chapter 13 appeared in a different version in The Art of Simple as "I practice simple living but I still love my stuff," https://www .theartofsimple.net/still-love-my-stuff/ on October 16, 2015. A portion of the story of Lazarus in Chapter 15 appeared in a different version in *Field Notes* newsletter on June 28, 2020. A small portion of the off-brand story in Chapter 16 appeared in a different version on Sarah Bessey's blog on May 4, 2016. A small portion of the yes-and story in Chapter 16 appeared in a different version in an Evolving Faith sermon on October 15, 2022. A portion of the story of Eucharist at the church appeared in a different version in *Field Notes* newsletter on April 26, 2021.

"Grateful acknowledgment is made to the following for permission to reprint previously published material:

THE CHARLOTTE SHEEDY LITERARY AGENCY: "Don't Hesitate" from *Swan* by Mary Oliver, copyright © 2010, 2017 by Mary Oliver. Reprinted with permission of Bill Reichblum and The Charlotte Sheedy Literary Agency.
BRIAN D. MCLAREN: "Four Stages of Faith Development" (original version can be found in *Faith After Doubt*). Reprinted with the permission of Brian D. McLaren.
THE INSTITUTE OF JESUIT SOURCES: "Patient Trust" by Pierre Teilhard de Chardin, SJ, from *Hearts on Fire: Praying With Jesuits,* copyright © 1993, 2004 by The Institute of Jesuit Sources. Reprinted with permission of The Institute of Jesuit Sources, Chestnut Hill, MA.

British Library Cataloguing-in-Publication Data
A catalogue record for this book is available from the British Library

ISBN 978-0-281-09029-7
eBook ISBN 978-0-281-09028-0

10 9 8 7 6 5 4 3 2 1

First printed in Great Britain by Clays Limited, Bungay, Suffolk

Produced on paper from sustainable forests

For B. Joan Styles: my esteemed mother, wise mentor, hilarious companion, tenacious protector, knitting addiction enabler, and beloved friend. I'll never get over the way that you've stayed in step our whole lives, in every evolution, with empathy and curiosity, all while growing, healing, and transforming your own self. Everything I know about love, God, motherhood, abundance, connection, and joy has its roots in you. I'm so grateful, Mum.

PATIENT TRUST

By Pierre Teilhard de Chardin, SJ

Above all, trust in the slow work of God.
We are quite naturally impatient in everything to reach the
    end without delay.
We should like to skip the intermediate stages.
We are impatient of being on the way to something
    unknown, something new.
And yet it is the law of all progress
that it is made by passing through some stages of instability—
and that it may take a very long time.
And so I think it is with you;
your ideas mature gradually—let them grow,
let them shape themselves, without undue haste.
Don't try to force them on,
as though you could be today what time
(that is to say, grace and circumstances acting on your own
    good will)
will make of you tomorrow.
Only God could say what this new spirit
gradually forming within you will be.
Give Our Lord the benefit of believing
that his hand is leading you,
and accept the anxiety of feeling yourself
in suspense and incomplete.

CONTENTS

Field Notes
for the
Wilderness

Chapter 1

WELCOME TO THE WILDERNESS

Dear Wanderer,

Welcome, welcome, my friend. Here you are, at the beginning. Isn't that a sacred place to be?

There are a lot of reasons why folks like us find ourselves in the wilderness. And right now, it's even feeling a bit crowded. We are in the midst of a shift in the Church that has resulted in many of us here, outside the city gates, exhausted and scared, sad and angry, and yet just a little relieved.

You don't have to have it all figured out right now. You aren't required to have all of the answers you seek when you aren't even quite certain of your own questions just yet. You certainly don't need to know where you will end up by the end of this experience. But being willing to begin takes great courage, especially when your heart is a bit battered and broken, when your story hasn't worked out the way you thought it would.

I've loved the metaphor of the wilderness for many years now. It just seems to fit with what I understand of the world and my place in it. If the city is a metaphor for certainty and belonging, then the wilderness is for our questions and our truth.

You wouldn't have picked up this book if you didn't understand the wilderness in some way. If you hadn't found yourself out here, beyond the city gates, on your own or with a ragtag little company of makeshift companions.

The wilderness can be a strange, disorienting, lonely place

for a soul, I know. It can be filled with danger and loss. But along the way, we do find each other. We come across little clearings, like this, where we can spread our quilt for a while, sit around the fire together, and share some time, maybe a thermos or two of tea.

I'm glad you're here by my quilt and campfire. You're so welcome here.

I DON'T KNOW WHAT PROPELLED you to embark on this journey. Some of us, like myself, very consciously found ourselves leaving the city and entering the wilderness because of our questions, our doubts, our but-what-about questions.* Others of us were never welcome in the city to begin with; the wilderness has been your primary address for as long as you can remember. You have much to teach us. However we found ourselves here, look up, look up, you can see the stars out here in a way you never could inside the city gates. You're not as alone as you feel.

This book is my own hopeful offering of what has served me in the wilderness, the practices and postures I have found to be good companions when danger feels close and losses have accumulated and loneliness a constant. The tools you actually

---

* It's worth noting that I am writing to you as someone who was made for that city of certainty and belonging. I mean, I'm a nice white lady who is married with kids. The "city" usually loves women like me. So when I left the city gates, it was on purpose and it was a choice in some ways. But for many of us, we never belonged in the city—maybe it's because of our sexuality or gender identity, maybe it's because we are not neurotypical, maybe because of how we were raised or how we look or our body, or how we move through the world. The city tends to value conformity, and for people like me, that's an actual possibility until it isn't. But for a lot of us, conformity isn't even possible and so the city was never our home, which is important to name.

need or eventually use might be different—because you're gloriously, wonderfully different from me. That's one of the reasons why I tend to steer clear of prescriptive advice and how-to manuals or instructions: you will discern what will serve you and what you can release without my interference. What I'm offering are the knowings I arrived at the hard way, through mistakes and missteps and outright failures. These are the practices I still embrace in my daily life, the things I wish I had known when my back felt the final close of the city gate behind me with nothing but wilderness ahead. I hope to simply be alongside you as a companion for this time.

Some of the practices might meet you right where you are. Others you'll remember in a few years when you need them. A few might not work for your own journey, and that's okay.

In a lot of ways, I may be writing the book I wish I would have had twenty years ago. Back then, I was in the early stages of what folks would now call "deconstruction," but back then? I had no such language. It was just after 9/11 and I was a young pastor's wife, a fish-out-of-water Canadian in south Texas, and everything I thought I knew about God was disappearing like campaign promises. In the years since then, I've spent a lot of time out here in the wilderness. This big sky and wide-open space have become a second home to me, even when I feel alone. It's here I discovered that the wilderness isn't a problem to be solved, it is another altar of intimacy with God. I never would have imagined that would be true all those years ago.

WATER IN THE LITERAL DESERT?

About twenty years ago, my husband and I were driving through Arizona, not quite halfway between our old life in

Texas and our new life back home in Canada, towing a seen-better-days U-Haul stuffed with our worldly goods.*

The August heat was radiating off the road, but we kept the windows open because our air conditioner was never able to keep up with the American Southwest. Hot air thundered into our Chevy, whipping my hair out of its ponytail; my legs were stuck to the seat. It felt like I had been hot for years, and maybe that was true. This Canadian gal had never managed to acclimate to the temperature properly. The years we spent in south Texas had been a bittersweet roller coaster with beauty and sorrow, devastation and joy. The one constant was my inability to handle the heat well.

Brian had just resigned from pastoral ministry, and we were limping home to Canada to reimagine our future, more than a little brokenhearted and burned out. Once idealistic, I had become cynical about fog machines and voter guides. Brian may have been the one to leave his Jesus-y job behind, but I was the one losing my faith altogether. We were still grieving our latest miscarriage and questioning many of our experiences in full-time vocational ministry and the ways we were taught—or expected—to be in the world. Everything I knew about God had become a gigantic question mark, and everything I thought about Christians had become a howl of betrayal and frustration.

The sky was blue, the horizon endless, our pain immense. We talked (okay, fine, I ranted) all the way across the red desert. My soul was as parched for water as the landscape around us.

God had once felt as near as my breath; now there was only space, space, space.

When we stopped for gas and lunch, I opened the car door

---

* Note: "worldly goods" in our case meant particleboard furniture and second-hand books.

and stepped onto the shimmering pavement, a river of perspiration snaking down my spine. "Ugh, I'm so sick of being hot!" I complained, tipping my head back in exhaustion.

"Have you ever considered that you're not having a spiritual crisis, and perhaps you've just been overheated? For many, *many* years?" asked my husband mildly, taking his life in his hands. I threw an empty water bottle at him and he laughed.

As Brian pumped gas, I bought water and hopefully-only-a-day-old sandwiches from the gas station store. He parked to the side of the station and then we followed crumbling signs pointing to a picnic table in a clump of scrubby trees along a ditch. We continued our conversation from the car.

"I feel like I'm wandering in a desert," I said, gesturing at the landscape around us. "I'm not who I used to be, but I'm not sure where I'm going next either. There isn't much out here but a lot of space. It's scary. Like who I was has disappeared. Like God has disappeared."

"That's fine." Brian was unbothered. "I figure God meets us in those places of space more than when we are pretending to have it all figured out or cram our souls full of our own opinions and certainties. I'm not worried."

But I was.

My fears weren't unfounded. I knew how it went. The system we were a part of operated best when we all knew our lines and followed the cues. If someone stepped out of line, the response was swift and often merciless: if you weren't "in," you were very, very out. And if you were on the outs, well, you didn't just lose your church, you lost your friends, your community, and in our case, even our source of income. The margin for error felt small because it was.

And I worried that Brian and I stood to lose not only our

vocation, our calling, the path of life we had prepared ourselves to follow, including our community and friends, but even each other. I worried that if I got it wrong, if I got God wrong, the consequences could be spectacular and eternal. I worried that church was an adventure in missing the point, yet I yearned for it as much as I was angry at it. I worried that God was angry at me. I worried that I was going to lose my faith, the thing that I was clinging to with white knuckles by now, like a kid trying to force last year's favorite shirt to fit after a growth spurt. I had always loved Jesus, was I losing Jesus? I worried that I would lose my family, my friends, my understanding of the world. I was scared of my anger and my grief, terrified of what I already knew, and begging myself not to know it. Every answer I had memorized had become inadequate. I wrung my soul's hands.

When we fell silent at the picnic table, we realized we were hearing something.

Was that . . . the sound of . . . *water*?

In the desert?

Our eyes met and we stood up, turning toward the sound. We walked to the ridge behind our picnic table and peered down what we had initially thought was just a crevasse: there were trees beneath us; their tops were at our feet. It was a hillside leading to a small, bright creek running at the bottom. We scrambled down the bank and farther into the trees that had been below our line of sight, lower and lower toward the river. We reached the edge of the laughing creek, skidding the last few steps.

Unthinking, I kicked off my dusty sandals and walked barefoot right into the water. The light came through the trees, and I could see clear to the bottom of the creek.

I knelt down, right into the red rock bed, and plunged my hands into the cool water, groaning aloud with pleasure. My swollen feet rejoiced.

Cupping my hands, I lifted the water to my own bowed head and opened my palms, allowing the water to run down the crown of my head, dripping along my hair and neck. Over and over, I baptized myself in the desert's water.

After what felt like an age, I finally looked back at the bank. Brian was perched on a rock with his own now-bare feet dangling in the water, watching me with a smile.

"Isn't a literal stream in the desert a bit too 'on the nose'?" I called.

"God's such a show-off," he said comfortably, leaning back.

I stood up, water running down my legs and dripping from my fingers. My hair and shirt were damp but already drying in the heat. This was just a small brook in the desert, hardly worth noticing to most people, hiding behind a humble roadside gas station.

But it felt like my first glimpse of something true. I had thought God was absent from me, but it turned out that a desert wasn't an absence of God. This journey was an invitation to a new path of intimacy and depth, growth and evolution. The wilderness wasn't something for me to fear: God was already here, making a way. When the old sacred spaces have been desecrated, and we find ourselves questioning whether we'll find home again, homemade baptisms are awaiting us in the wilderness.

"All right, I'm ready to keep going," I said. We got back in the Chevy and headed north, following the desert road all the way to our new home.

DECONSTRUCTION, UNDEFINED

In the early 2000s, deconstruction was a distinctly lonely experience. I got online around that time but didn't really find community until the mid-to-late aughts. Conversations about Biblical literalism, feminism, and atonement theory were happening in academic and seminary settings but not in our regular old churches, you know?

So there was a fair amount of pearl clutching and panic from folks around me as I questioned and pushed back and flailed and raged. My experience didn't feel as methodical or thoughtful as the word "deconstruction" implies: it felt like kicking down every edifice I ever built for God and dancing on the ashes of old fires. It felt like flying and like falling, sometimes at the same moment.

Philosopher Jacques Derrida introduced the notion that meaning changes and it isn't empirically settled. We're always evolving in how we understand words and texts, and the meaning of those words. The notion of deconstruction—of taking the accepted idea or truth and then pulling it apart to explore its evolving truth, complexity, and meaning—has become part of our cultural landscape. In this book, we're focused on a particular sort of religion—western-influenced evangelicalism and her surroundings—but deconstruction is also a conversation in history, sociology, psychology, literature, LGBTQ+ conversations, social justice work, feminist and womanist studies, and even art, music, architecture, and beyond. There aren't too many areas of the human experience that have escaped conversations on deconstruction: pulling at the accepted truths to tease out "the thing-under-the-thing" in an effort toward deeper truth and understanding.

But in faith spaces, "deconstruction" is one of those words

that has almost ceased to have much meaning beyond what the person using the word implies. At the most basic level, we begin our life of faith in a mode of "construction"—meaning we're building our beliefs and foundations for life. Deconstruction, then, implies that there comes a time when we begin to pull that faith "structure" apart to see what's underneath it. Sometimes this leads to a reconstruction of belief, resulting in a stronger, more robust, inclusive, and loving form of faith. Sometimes it leads to deconversion altogether. And sometimes it leads us back to where we began after all. I've seen folks talk about deconstruction like it's the devil's own work and an excuse to sin. Others talk about it as the apex possibility of faith, like only the really serious and thoughtful people deconstruct. There are those who see the conclusion as foregone, a loss of faith; others as a deepening of it. To some it's a threat, others a risk, an act of faith, possibly that proverbial slippery slope of which we were warned. It can be all of that and none of that. But it has gotten to the point where some of us cringe when we hear the word "deconstruction" because there is so much misunderstanding and misrepresentation of those of us who have engaged in this hard and holy work.

I don't mind the term "deconstruction," not really. I figure whatever language helps you feel seen or affirmed or serves you during the process is yours to discover or embrace and bless or reject. Some folks prefer "reimagining" or "renovation" or "reformation" or even "faith shift"—I see the benefits and the limits of each. I've used them all myself now and then, and we probably will use a few of them during our time together.

Personally, I have always liked the word "evolving," as it helps me to do what Father Richard Rohr calls "transcend and include" my faith experiences both before that season and since. As my dear friend Rachel Held Evans once said, "An evolving faith is simply faith that has adapted in order to survive."[1]

Yet the word "deconstruction" can imply a one-and-done experience to me. In our metaphor, it implies that the wilderness is a brisk walk, quickly solved and resolved. It promises a linear journey. It's filled with tips and tricks and guides, coaches and navigable maps. It seems like an event.

But an *evolving* faith? To me, an evolving faith is never simply about "deconstruction." It has proven to be about the questions, the curiosity, and the ongoing reckoning of a robust, honest faith. An evolving faith brings the new ideas and ancient paths together. It's about rebuilding and reimagining a faith that works not only for ourselves but for the whole messy, wide, beautiful world. For me, this has proven to be deeply centered in the Good News of Jesus. An evolving faith is sacramental, ecumenical, embodied, generous, spirit-filled, truthful, and rooted in the unconditional, never-ending love of God. It isn't a linear experience of one and done and dusted. An evolving faith is a resilient and stubborn form of faithfulness that is well acquainted with the presence of God in our loneliest places and deepest questions. And an evolving faith has room for all the paths you may navigate after our time together in these pages.

Anyone who gets to the end of their life with the exact same beliefs and opinions they had at the beginning is doing it wrong.[2] Because if we don't change and evolve over our lifetime, then I have to wonder if we're paying attention to the invitation of the Holy Spirit that is your life. Lisa Sharon Harper says that pilgrimage is about transformation.[3] An evolving faith is a form of pilgrimage, and so yes, you are being transformed.

ROLL CALL

When I cast my eye around our quilt next to the campfire here, I can see those of us who are here because our churches became a never-ending political rally for a single particular ideology, usually one that didn't bear any resemblance to the brown-skinned Jesus who taught us to love our neighbors and our enemies. For instance, if your politics and your faith were so entwined as to be one and the same, disentangling that knot can feel exhausting and impossible, yet necessary.

And welcome to the vast company of those of us with unanswered prayers. Or those of us who were in vocational ministry but burned out, or who had to hide our questions because our paycheck depended on it, or who experienced spiritual abuse by the ones we trusted.

Some of us are here because we are disabled or sick or chronically ill. So we are often ignored or judged or pitied or reduced to a prayer request—or, worst of all, invited to join a multilevel marketing scheme for essential oils.

I'm tender for those of us who had nightmares as little kids about judgment day because of movies or hell houses designed to scare people into heaven and so you "got saved" a minimum of six times just in case the first five didn't count. Traumatizing children was a regular get-them-saved-young tactic. (The eighties and nineties were *wild*, folks, and I haven't even mentioned the Satanic Panic.)

There are those of us who burned or threw out our secular CDs in an effort to be holy. We'll never get that Tragically Hip or Janet Jackson album back, but it's fine—that's why God gave us Spotify.

A rueful smile for all of us who did everything right and yet everything went wrong because it turns out, life isn't a recipe to follow and someone's interpretation of the Bible isn't a blueprint, and prayer isn't a vending machine, and faith isn't a synonym for control, and Scripture isn't an answer book, and the scripts we were given fell flat.

Welcome to those of us who didn't so much "cross a threshold into the wilderness" as much as fell, body and soul, into the wasteland from the hospital or the divorce court or the graveside or the church committee to "explore gender and sexuality." There's room for those of us who were devastated by our church's stance on LGBTQ+ inclusion. We learned to hide ourselves out of fear.

There are many of us who lost someone we loved and found that there wasn't room for our grief at church. Or the sorrow and rage we still feel for George Floyd and Breonna Taylor and the Highway of Tears and Uvalde and how we all know that I could keep listing names and places, and even that makes us as sad as we are furious.

There are a lot of us who have good memories and grateful associations and healthy families who were human, yes, but loving and kind—precisely because of their faith—but still we somehow found that the script wasn't working anymore and our questions had taken over, and now the things that used to make sense suddenly feel pointless, even absurd.

A gentle welcome to those who have experienced religion only through colonization and abuse and loss for seven generations and beyond, let alone the complications of legacy within our cultures, community diasporas, and family stories.

Some of us landed here because we were blamed for mental illness and told to pray more, or were hurt or abused in the places where we should have been safest. And just for the record, let's go ahead and rebuke conversion therapy, in the name of Jesus.

Hello to all those who deeply regret their short-term mission trips; or broke up with a girlfriend because it was time to date Jesus; or whose parents gave them a purity ring; or who faithfully followed the probably-tax-exempt-status-disqualifying voter guide at the election; or who protested at an abortion clinic they later secretly visited. Some of us landed here because our heroes turned out to be more fallible and broken than we can bear.

Welcome to all of us who have lost friends and family and every sense of belonging we ever had. It turned out that what we thought was love was actually mutually agreed upon like-mindedness. Some of us landed here because everything we had hoped to find at church we found instead at a pride parade or an Alcoholics Anonymous meeting or a gentle parenting support group or therapy. For what it's worth, I'm so glad you found that.

There are so many ways we've had our hearts broken and our hopes dashed and our trust shattered. We dared to show up anyway, and we keep hanging on to this Story with which we're all continuing to wrestle.

God, you're courageous.

And you aren't alone.

I AM NOT AFRAID FOR YOU

The temptation when you've found yourself here in the wilderness is to run for the nearest shelter of certainty you can find. We can find those shelters in online communities, in new friendships, in causes, in new-to-us beliefs and doctrines. I get that. I think that's why so many of us end up becoming progressive versions of our former fundamentalist selves for a while there. We're still just as certain, just as committed to litmus tests, desperate for answers to who is in and who is out, looking for a fight to prove our faithfulness.

In some ways, when we find ourselves in the wilderness, we're urgently hustling to escape it again. So we turn toward guides who promise us certainty and healing. There is no shortage of experts in the wilderness. There are even a few carnival barkers out here. There will be those promising shortcuts and quick fixes, selling superiority out of the back of a van. Be suspicious of this. Your instincts might be rusty from disuse, but you'll get the hang of your own heart again. It's okay if you need to try what the experts and influencers are selling for a while, most of us do. But sooner or later we find ourselves here again because the invitation was never to a more progressive form of the old you or a tidy set of answers or a new mediator between you and Jesus. The invitation was never going to be to a chipper plan, goal-setting worksheet, positive affirmations and do-better mantras that fit into an Instagram square. It's always been about the love of God, for and in you, and also for and in this beautiful tragedy of the world. It will always be homemade, not store bought.

Here at the beginning of our time together, I simply want to bless and normalize what you're feeling. You're not broken. You're not bad. You're not in need of a stronger hand and tighter boundaries. You're not wrong, nor are you doing something wrong.

One thing that my dad told me when I was at the beginning stages of my own deconstruction has become the hallmark of my work in this arena, particularly with Evolving Faith.* In response to my very real and legitimate fears of where this wilderness wandering and questioning would lead me, he told me something along the lines of this: "I'm not afraid for you. If you're honestly seeking God, I believe you will find what you're looking for, even if it looks different than what I have found."

I still remember the whooshing exhale my relieved soul experienced at his words, like the lifting of a burden that wasn't mine to carry anyway. It was permission to evolve, and it was love. And so, all these years later, I have adopted that as my own approach to those who are on a winding path of spiritual growth and formation—*be not afraid.*

I'm not afraid for those who are wondering and wandering. I'm not afraid for them or of them, for you or of you. I still believe the Apostle Paul who wrote in his letter to the Romans that "neither death nor life, neither angels nor demons, neither the present nor the future, nor any powers, neither height nor depth, nor anything else in all creation, will be able to separate us from the love of God that is in Christ Jesus our Lord."†

We are often told that only those of us who are faithless end up here in the wilderness, that if you were really a true believer you wouldn't have found yourself here or that this is all an elaborate scheme to justify "sinful behavior." Beloved, nothing could be further from the truth. As poet Christian Wiman writes, "Sometimes God calls a person to unbelief in order that faith may take new forms."4 You're likely here because you were

---

* I cofounded Evolving Faith with my friends Rachel Held Evans and Jim Chaffee. It's since become a thriving online community as well as a yearly conference for folks like us who find themselves in the wilderness of faith. You can learn more at https://evolvingfaith.com.
† Romans 8:38–39, NIV.

the true believer kid. You were the one who took it seriously, weren't you? In my experience, and in the experience of walking alongside many others wandering out here, I can say with some measure of authority that you're in a very normal, very healthy stage of faith, and you're likely exactly where you're supposed to be right now. I believe the wilderness is an invitation from the Holy Spirit, a gorgeous, rowdy invitation to the life you never dreamed possible, a more welcoming sort of party with a few quiet corners for good conversation. It seems to me that we're desperate for some gentleness, compassion, wide-open space, and kindness.

GENEROUS GENTLENESS

When you cross these sorts of thresholds, you are often inundated with well-meaning folks (like me) who overwhelm you with books, resources, podcasts, essays, and practices designed for the outcome we desire for you. I mean, I have yet to find a problem I won't throw twelve books at, so I get it. Those resources can and often do serve us very beautifully, but they can also be another attempt at controlling our thoughts, our behaviors, our outcomes. What you really need is trust, patience, honor for your doubts and your questions, along with radical acceptance.

You are deeply loved and God is not worried about you. You can rest and abide in that Love even as you throw a few things into the fire.

Jesus once said, "Come close to my side, you whose hearts are on the ground, you who are pushed down and worn out, and I will refresh you. Follow my teachings and learn from me, for I am gentle and humble of heart, and you will find rest from your troubled thoughts. Walk side by side with me and I will share in your heavy load and make it light.'*

You who are pushed down and worn out. You whose hearts are on the ground. That's us, isn't it?

Few of us enter the wilderness like it's a parade or a party. Usually we enter with our hearts on the ground, pushed down and worn out. That invitation of rest and gentleness, of journeying with Jesus in the wilderness, is likely the exhale you're craving.

The first thing we need to learn in the wilderness is generous gentleness. Toward ourselves. Toward the old versions of ourselves. Toward those around us. Toward the universe eventually. Toward the holy work of our own life. The wilderness isn't your place for striving, not really.

THERE ARE A DOZEN THINGS I want to press into your hands while I have you here, but the first invitation I want to offer to you is this: be gentle with yourself. Some of the work you're about to do here in the wilderness will be evident to people. Other work will be evident only to you, perhaps your therapist or your closest people or just the Spirit. It's all going to be good work, I believe, and I bless you in it. But this is also the place to begin with gentleness.

Gentle with your expectations. Gentle with your demands. Gentle with your soul and your story. Gentle with your partner, your kids, your people. Gentle with your needs, your wants, your desires. Gentle with your good heart, curious mind, and your beloved body.

---

* Matthew 11:28–30, First Nations Translation.

You're learning that you don't have to earn your own joy and belonging. You're learning that you're beloved by God, our Mother, and you're learning to let God love you as a good mother would love you. You're learning how to love the world again. You're learning you are worthy of love and wholeness, too.

INVITATIONS FROM JESUS

Just before Brian and I stumbled across that oasis in the desert in Arizona, my dad had sent me that same passage of Scripture in Matthew I just mentioned. (He's been in the habit of doing that for most of my life, sending along a verse or phrase from the Bible that might encourage or strengthen or comfort.)

In that moment, I was at the threshold of the wilderness for the first time in my life and it terrified me. Many of us know that passage of Scripture from the more traditional translations, which read something similar to "Come to me, all you who are weary and burdened, and I will give you rest. Take my yoke upon you and learn from me, for I am gentle and humble in heart, and you will find rest for your souls. For my yoke is easy and my burden is light." But my dad decided to send me Eugene Peterson's *The Message* translation of the verses.

Are you tired? Worn out? Burned out on religion? Come to me. Get away with me and you'll recover your life. I'll show you how to take a real rest. Walk with me and work with me—watch how I do it. Learn the unforced rhythms of grace. I won't lay anything heavy or ill-fitting on you. Keep company with me and you'll learn to live freely and lightly.

As the years unfolded I kept returning to those words from Jesus. And with each reading, I began to see the invitations of Jesus as making room for an evolving faith and how this passage could be a path to follow.

First, I was struck by hearing that Jesus acknowledges our weariness and our burden, friends. Jesus doesn't judge the burdened one for the burden or the sad one for the sadness or the disappointed one for the disappointment or the brokenhearted one for the grief. Jesus doesn't say to you, "If you were more faithful, you wouldn't feel like that! This is your fault—you need more quiet times, you need more work, more Bible studies, more prayer, more YouTube deep dives, more faith, you deserve this suffering, you need to put others first more! Squash those doubts and complexities! Ignore your unanswered questions and quiet devastations."

Rather, there is a tenderness to Jesus's words here. God acknowledges, even blesses, your weariness. It turns out that, yes, the yoke *has* been too heavy. It's not all in your head.

POOR WEE LAMB

When our four kids were just wee tinies, I found that when they were distraught or upset or hurt that it helped if I simply reflected back to them what they were feeling, almost as a validation. It could be as simple as "You want to stay at the park, you're sad that we have to go." Or "You fell and hurt yourself, it really hurts, you poor lamb." Even "You are mad because you wanted to play with that toy. I can see that." Hiccups and snotty noses and tears usually turned toward rest, toward calm or resolution, toward their mum's arms. The relief of being understood, of having their feelings named opened up the room for the possibility of moving forward.

This approach can seem counterintuitive. Most of us have an instinct to correct, reason, distract, or (my personal favorite) aggressively cheer up. If you need a silver lining to be found, I'm your gal. No one has ever magically become fine simply because they are told "You're fine, it's fine, everything's fine." But I promise that is not for my lack of effort.

Yet I saw in those years how the then-tinies relaxed when I named and affirmed their experience in recognition of their suffering: *Yes, you are sad; yes, this hurts; yes, I can name with you what you feel and love you in it.* I remember how they leaned in, craving my acknowledgment of their pain, that naming, before they could even begin to turn toward healing or rising.

Telling the truth is its own holy comfort. The wilderness gives you room for the satisfaction of simply naming things as they are—including yourself. It's Mother God's arms holding you as you admit that you and this world are not fine, in order to be able to rise in faith, in hope, in justice, toward the co-creation of making things right . . . eventually. Just not yet.

When my children were little and would experience those minor bumps and bruises of growing up, I would bundle them up into my arms and say, "Oh, you poor wee lamb." I used to say it with grandiose affection, an overabundance of sympathy in a Scottish accent,* and inevitably they would laugh and cheer up. But by the time our youngest was born, it had become a tender phrase whispered in times of grief and pain. While my hand smoothed their hair from a feverish forehead or sat at their bedside while we debriefed a hard day.

---

* My mother's family is originally from Scotland, and so that accent comes naturally to our house.

One day when she was only two, our youngest daughter, Maggie, was with her babysitter and she had a little fall on the sidewalk, scraping her knees and the palms of her hands. After work, when I came to pick her up, she was sitting happily and playing without a care. But when she saw me? Oh, she turned to me, bottom lip quivering, arms up, eyes filled with tears, and said, "Mummy, would you please call me a poor wee lamb?"

So perhaps because I'm a mother of four, that passage in Matthew reads to me like God as a mother whispering, joining us in acknowledging our pain, naming it with us, as well as giving us a path to life.

And I'm not only talking about the doubts, our fears, our cynicism, our disbelief, our questions. Those things are real and are often what first awaken us to the exhaustion and sadness of our times.

But I believe Jesus is also talking about the burdens that are not simply internal but external. So Jesus was also calling out the heavy yoke that the religious elite or the powerful or our culture often placed upon us. The burden isn't imaginary—it's a burden to bear, when we see so many of our generation falling prey to and baptizing the powers and principalities of the age like Christian nationalism, fearfulness, dehumanization, religion as measuring stick of worthiness, racism, cruelty, patriarchy, homophobia—these are real and devastating burdens. It's not your imagination, friend.

And so it's good and healing to name that. Mother God acknowledges your grief, your burden, your pain, your weariness today. It's okay to rest in that for a while. Allow yourself a moment to see God crouched down beside you whispering, "I see that you are sad. I see that you are tired. I see that you are weary. I see that this burden has been too great to bear on your own. You're not wrong to feel burdened; it is and has been a burden to you. And I am here."

COME AWAY WITH ME

After acknowledgment of your burden, I love that Jesus says, "Come away with me." Walk with me, work with me—watch how I do it.

During my seasons of deconstruction and rebuilding, it felt like the more I learned about Jesus, the more I began to realize that God was even better than I could have imagined. I even started to get mad, asking my husband and the whole Internet if everyone else knew how amazing this Jesus guy really was.

I began to see the subversiveness of Jesus, long tamed, interpreted away, and inoculated. Jesus was embodying a real rest, unforced rhythms of grace. God was taking naps when God was tired, taking time to pray alone, feeding the hungry, aligning with the poor and oppressed, honoring children, eating with sex workers and sinners, teaching women and including them among his disciples, washing the feet of his followers, calming storms, laying down his life, and rising again. Jesus was giving us a glimpse of what it means to live fully within the love of God—it looked like freedom and wholeness and an unforced rhythm of grace.

That invitation to walk with Jesus became breath and life to me. I always say it was following Jesus that made a feminist out of me.* But it was also following Jesus that made me care about

---

* That's basically the whole premise of my first book, *Jesus Feminist*.

justice, about politics and theology, about pronouns and fiscal policy, about maternal health care justice and refugees, about good food and remembering to sing sometimes. It was following Jesus that compelled me to begin this lifelong process of decolonizing my faith, to grapple with my privilege, to embark on rooting out white supremacy not only from my own faith but from the structures and systems of my faith, too. It was following Jesus that led me to pray for my enemies instead of curse them, that led me to love the ones I used to despise, that reminded me that no longer were we called servants but instead God called us friends.

This is an unforced rhythm of grace.

And why? Because the God I met in the wilderness reawakened me, recovered me, restored me to the Gospel of Love. This is the Gospel as I learned it at the feet of Jesus, hanging on to the hem of his humble garment. The width, length, height, and depth of God's love is not fearful or restrictive or small or dull. It is a wide-open, sharp love that sets us free. It is a love that never steals, kills, or destroys us—it came that we might have life, and life that is more abundant.* It is this love that brings us rest, that lifts burdens, that restores souls, that opens hearts, and changes lives.

It turned out that what I thought was the wilderness was actually God's grace and goodness. What I thought was exile became home, and the misfits became my friends. What I thought was a dead religion with nothing to offer me but more burdens became a practice of faith that connected me not only to God but to my neighbor. What I thought was the wilderness turned into a homecoming.

* John 10:10.

LET'S TALK EXPECTATIONS

In the past ten years or so, I've had the privilege of walking alongside other folks who are working through their own evolving faith. We find each other in the hallways of churches or at conferences, in the parking lot at my kids' school or through long emails that arrive in my inbox. Over the years, I've cobbled together a few principles or postures that I hope will serve you well in the wilderness, not as a new version of old ways—or new wine in old wineskins, perhaps—but as adaptable wisdom that leaves room for you to stretch out and explore the Love of God for yourself. After all, more than cramming ourselves into someone else's answers, we actually need permission, grace, and space to rise to our own soul's full height.

This isn't much of a rule book—rules rarely belong in the wilderness—but more of a field guide, a companion of sorts. Even theologically, I won't have a lot of answers here for you; there are many good guides on the particulars of what you're grappling with—from how church should or shouldn't look to how to raise your kids, from rearranging your thoughts on sex to finding a new path for faith. I encourage you to honor your search for specifics; what I'm offering you is mostly companionship, the hope to help you adapt and survive in your journey even as it differs from my own.

I also want to offer a gentle content warning before you proceed, because you will encounter references to abuse, miscarriage, racism, infant loss, death, and other topics some readers may find upsetting. Please care for yourself well by going slow, taking breaks as needed, or even skipping some sections if you need to.

A field guide tends to be a little more informal, meant to be tucked into a back pocket or folded into a backpack or a jacket pocket so you can bring it along for the journey. Tuck many of these ideas into your own back pocket, eh? The notion of being prescriptive, of taking the things that work for me and the things I believe, and making them into some universal rule makes me queasy. Some of these practices will serve you well; others might be for someone else. I've also prepared a guided journal for you as a companion to this book so that you have the opportunity to reflect on and rework some of these principles for your own lived experience.

So let's begin, shall we? After many years of navigating the wilderness myself and hosting little feasts here at the bonfire for fellow wanderers, I can offer you these few things I know.

Or at least, I think I know them. For now.

I'm glad you're here,
S.

Chapter 2

AN EVOLVING FAITH IS
ANOTHER WAY THROUGH

Dear Wonderer,

I remember the moment I finally lost my old pathways altogether. Twenty years later, I can still feel the cobblestone streets of Bonn under my feet, the press of people flowing past me as I stood like a stone in their river of movement. I was in the midst of another miscarriage and far from home. My husband and I longed for this particular baby, and days before, as the signs of loss began to accumulate, I faithfully deployed all the methods and formulas of prayer in my arsenal.

Basically, I named and claimed all the things.

I came of age in a segment of Christianity known as the prosperity gospel. In my world, prayer was a means of controlling outcomes. Oh, we didn't frame it quite as baldly as that, but I wonder now if that wasn't the subtext. The bigger the faith, the bigger the "blessing" (which almost always meant health and material wealth). Sometimes we shouted Bible verses to remind God of their out-of-context promises in Scripture and called it praying. I was taught to pray like an overcomer, demand like a victor, and expect miracles as a birthright.*

I still remember that moment on the street because it was the moment when I finally, mercifully, stopped.

We were on a mission trip of all things. My husband was

---

* Thanks, Oral Roberts!

a youth pastor at the time, and we were there with about twenty-five teenagers engaging in dance troupes and street art performance, preaching at local churches, and developing cross-cultural friendships, with the aim of evangelizing local teens. Bless. I was never the one in front preaching or leading, much more content to be the one keeping track of passports and curfews. Days before we left, my doctor had informed me that my pregnancy was ending. She had recommended a procedure to resolve the inevitable safely, but me? I had full expectations of a miracle. I got on the plane with those kids, convinced that God was going to surprise everyone. (Except for me. I wouldn't be surprised. I looked forward to my triumphant testimony: "I never wavered! I knew God is a God of miracles!" Et cetera.) Who else would *contend* for this pregnancy? No one, I reasoned. And so I began to contend in the only ways I knew how.*

In the lead-up to that moment on the street, I had deployed every tool in my arsenal. I wrote Bible verses on index cards and taped them to my mirror. I stopped listening to secular music; no more Radiohead, only K-Love while we're engaged in the serious business of petitioning heaven in prayer, you know? I lined up my confession—which is Word-of-Faith speak for never saying your deepest fears and worries out loud, only speaking words of faith and hope and certainty. *You're not sick, you're coming down with a healing!* I bound things on earth and loosed things in heaven through prayer. I fasted, I wept. I read my Bible and begged for prayer from the saints. I anointed everything, including myself, with oil. I *expected* a miracle.

---

* Even my default to the word "contend" was evidence of my double-down on what I knew to do. Contending in prayer is old Pentecostal-adjacent language for intercession; it implies the grappling and wrestling with the Spirit.

And still, days later, despite my "faithfulness," I was losing the baby. My bleeding wouldn't stop. My hormone levels weren't doubling. The miscarriage was taking an excruciatingly long time to complete. At night, Brian and I clung to each other in our narrow bed at the pension, quietly crying even while holding ourselves to the only course we knew, a course of faith and certainty and answered prayers.

On that day, we had a bit of time to spend in Bonn between events, so we set the kids free in a market on the cobblestone streets. They peered at necklaces and cherries, haggled over sausages. "I think, in Germany, the bun is just a handle for the sausage," one boy mused in admiration. I walked a little way away and stood alone for a time.

Sometimes reality comes to us slowly, in a dawning realization. Other times, we are whomped right into the real world, where we struggle for footing even as the great and terrible knowledge we've always known was there comes to light.

That moment was mine.

I simply stopped, right then and there, and admitted it was over now. The loss of that baby was a revelation of grief and longing that opened my eyes in a way books and sermons never could. I became part of the vast company of people with unanswered prayers.

THE THING UNDER THE THING

I've learned by now that most of us cross that threshold to the wilderness because of our grief. Oh, we'll call it a lot of other things, like anger or justified rage or doubt. We'll talk about political betrayals and disappointments with leadership. We'll say it's for a million reasons before we'll admit we are also sad,

sad, sad to our bones. That we're disappointed and grieving. However we got here or why, we've arrived on the other side of the city gates with our sorrow as lonely company.

Mine was an ordinary, quite common grief, but it was the cumulative tipping point just the same. And I'm not alone, I know.

Sometimes one of the greatest gifts God gives to us is losing our religion. We have to be committed to unlearning the unhelpful, broken, false, or incomplete things if we want to have space to relearn the goodness, joy, and embrace of God.[1]

But it sure doesn't feel like it at the time.

BURN IT DOWN OR DOUBLE DOWN

For those of us who were raised in or taught a version of faith that leans heavily into control and certainty, the first response to tension or challenge is often a posture I've come to call "doubling down." As it was originally used in the card game blackjack, "double down" meant a player being so confident in their hand and the outcome that they decide to double their bet.* When the odds are stacked against you, you work twice as hard and believe even harder.

When I think of my seasons of doubling down, I realize they were almost always guided by a deep desire for security and comfort and outcomes. My response to the miscarriage is exhibit A. In the face of uncertainty and pain, I returned to what had worked in the past or what was working for others around me, and then just did it better, higher, stronger, faster, more

---

* I mean, it also could mean the Kentucky Fried Chicken sandwich that includes fried chicken and bacon and then more fried chicken in the function of a bun, but for our purposes, doubling down is, unfortunately, not chicken-related.

than ever. Give me those Bible studies with unfurling flowers on the cover! Give me another worksheet to fill out! I'll stop asking questions. I'll be here at the church every time the doors are open. I'll tithe more than ten percent because the really serious ones tithe based on gross, not net income, right? I'll listen to the news channel you want, I'll read another book by another celebrity pastor, I'll take notes when Pastor* is preaching, I'll say things like "everything happens for a reason" and "all things work together for those who trust God." Anything that I've been told was a way toward peace, fulfillment, answered prayers, or certainty will become the blueprint. Surely if I double down on this, I'll be fine again. Surely my discomfort or my doubts or my grief will be solved by my faithfulness. God is always faithful, God is always good, and so the problem must be me, right?

But this posture has a shelf life. It can't go on forever. At a certain point all the things we're stuffing down, all the performances we're enacting, begin to ring hollow. And we find ourselves on a street in Bonn, bleeding and alone and finally ready to tell the truth. Or so I've heard.

AFTER RETURNING FROM GERMANY, I was angry. I'm not sure even now if I was angry at myself or angry at God or angry at my tradition and church—but oh, I was angry. Like most women raised in church, I was unacquainted with my own anger. I'd been taught for so long that it wasn't trustworthy, that it might even be sinful and unforgiving. I didn't know how to be angry very well; I had never learned, and so I flailed.

---

* Anyone else go to churches where a ministerial title somehow became a proper name? Totally normal.

In addition to our losing our baby, our church where Brian worked was locked in crisis at the time. I don't write or speak about this season of our life very often because it's a complicated story that involves a lot of people whom I still love and respect, but let me be honest with you, it was awful. Secrets were coming to the light, abuse and affairs were being revealed, political maneuvering was under way, sides were being taken. It's a tale as old as time for some of us.

I was barely twenty-five when I had a realization that of the multiple churches in the last ten years of my life, almost every single one had a pastor who had been involved in some form of sexual misconduct, if not outright abuse. Almost every single one. I'm in my mid-forties now, and that list has only gotten longer and more devastating. Some of those have been high-profile leaders in the Church; others were simply friends or acquaintances unknown to most; some I knew personally; others were simply strangers whose work I admired once.*

Sometimes that gap between our ideals about church and our experiences within the realities of church can just break your heart, you know?

And so I decided I needed to burn it all down.

I'M NOT ALONE IN THIS. Many of us turn from the double-down to the burn-it-down. Perhaps we imagine ourselves to be Angela Bassett in *Waiting to Exhale,* coolly walking away from

---

* The #ChurchToo movement was launched by Emily Joy Allison on Twitter, in response to the #MeToo movement, as acknowledgment that the place of abuse for many of us has been the Christian community. Since then, she has written *#ChurchToo: How Purity Culture Upholds Abuse and How to Find Healing.* There are multiple survivor groups, resources, and healing spaces that have developed in the past few years as well.

the cheating husband's car as it burns behind us. (Just me?) In reality, burning it down tends to manifest as a lot of crying, loneliness, disorientation, and ranting on social media. (Again, just me?)

We start to think that nothing is redeemable. Religion is a farce. Churches are full of abusers. We have been wounded and we fight back with everything in us. In some ways, we are still black-and-white thinkers, so we crave a villain and a simple enemy. To be fair, sometimes villainy abounds.

Eventually, I couldn't call myself a Christian anymore. I didn't go to church. I was pretty sure that I liked Jesus, but I didn't want much to do with institutional religion or what one of my teenagers now calls "the fan club." I questioned every-thing. I pushed back constantly. Even the smallest thing was a crossroad of rethinking and frustration. I saw only the negative and the damage. I hyperfixated on people with whom I dis-agreed and dedicated myself to the counterbalance, especially on social media and in elaborate arguments in my own head.

The burn-it-down phase is where a lot of us land for a long time. Some might stay there forever. It has benefits, but the cumulative effect over time leaves us hollowed out. We can burn it down until the earth is scorched to nothing and we are still hungry.

We often assume that these responses, doubling down or burning it down, are the only two options available to us at the threshold to the wilderness. And we might need to try them both on a time or two to figure out that they aren't the only options, nor are they necessarily the healthiest over the long term. But I've learned we don't have to choose between dou-bling down or burning it all down. There is another path in the wilderness, and it's the one I've become more interested in over the years, because I see a lot of possibilities for wholeness and integration there.

It's the path of an evolving faith.

AN EVOLVING FAITH ISN'T MADE FOR TV

After ministry, my husband went into the home restoration business. One of his biggest pet peeves is still reserved for those home renovation shows that depict an absolutely bonkers demolition day. The laughing crew goes into a house with a dated kitchen, for instance, and then wildly swings the sledgehammer in abandon through glass windows and full walls. Splinters flying, perfectly fine cupboards that could be donated to Habitat for Humanity ReStores destroyed, asbestos remediation ignored, electrical systems unmanaged, safety gear disregarded. Sure, it's for television, but he can hardly bear to watch the recklessness. In his experience, home restoration begins with thoughtful removal, taking into account the dangers and possibilities, with a dedicated and trained team. It's a precise and slow process, focused on renewal.

My deconstruction looked a lot more like the flying sledgehammers and a haphazard dumpster on the front lawn, stuffed willy-nilly with a mix of precious things and garbage at the same time.

There are some homes—and beliefs—that deserve the burn-it-down treatment, absolutely. But now that I've witnessed Brian and his team work over the years, I've seen how rare that approach really is in reality. Even when I think there isn't anything worth saving in a home, they are often able to see the foundation or the character or the possibilities. There is so much that love and care can heal.

After a fire or a flood or some other type of devastation to a home, Brian's team sweeps in to begin their work. But before they can start building again, they must pull out everything that's contaminated and damaged. They start by identifying all that's been ruined. The best possible thing they can do for the homeowner is to find every bit of fire and smoke and water and rot. Those places, if left unchecked, will poison the whole home—even if someday the walls are painted a lovely greige* and the countertops are sparkling. The removal of damage will always be a slow, methodical, careful process with cleaning as they go. It looks bad at the beginning. In the middle, it looks even worse. And then it begins to come together. The vision comes to life and the home is restored.

Basically, it is a whole sermon.

"THROUGH" CAN FEEL LIKE
A TERRIBLE WORD

One of the things we often deconstruct is the allure of a linear model of faith that says your life was always meant to be a strict progression from A to B, with requisite milestones, litmus tests, and boundary markers.

That was a nice fairy tale while it lasted, wasn't it? By now you've learned the hard way that life is less about if-this-then-that certainties than it is a gorgeous and frustrating improvisation with missteps and joys as we grow up and into who we were meant to be all along. We all begin somewhere different, and your journey won't be the same as mine (if you're lucky).

Let your story be yours. Let your evolving faith be your own.

---

* Greige is, I'm sad to say, a portmanteau word for gray + beige.

Let God meet you in the particular goodness of you, not a printer copy of someone else's best-case scenario for your life.

For those of us who were given a version of faith that celebrated and affirmed simplicity and certainty, the experience of being in the wilderness is profoundly unsettling and disorienting. Surely if we were more faithful or better Christians we wouldn't end up feeling as confused and out of sorts as we feel now, right?

Rather, it turns out that this is actually a healthy part of your spiritual formation. You're not doing it wrong. Maybe you just weren't ever told this, so let me say it plainly: you are loved by God in the wilderness because you've always belonged in Love. You'll make peace with your evolutions and journey, even the old versions of you that make you cringe sometimes to remember. There is a path through the wilderness but it's just that: *through*.

In the Gospel of John, Jesus healed a man who was born blind, and the religious leaders wanted to investigate this claim. During their questioning, Jesus responds to them with a story about a shepherd and a thief: the thief is trying to steal sheep, but they won't follow him out of the gate because they know only their beloved shepherd's voice. At first glance, you'd think that this means Jesus is the shepherd and he's keeping his sheep safe. But he goes on to tell the leaders that he is both the gate . . . and the shepherd. "I'll be explicit, then. I am the Gate for the sheep . . . Anyone who goes through me will be cared for—will freely go in and out, and find pasture . . . I am the Good Shepherd . . . I know my own sheep and my own sheep know me."* It is within this passage that we encounter another

---

* Excerpts from John 10:7–14 in *The Message,* paraphrase.

well-known teaching of Jesus's. He tells the crowd, "A thief is only there to steal and kill and destroy. I came so they can have real and eternal life, more and better life than they ever dreamed of."*

That last sentence deeply framed how my mother viewed God—through a lens of abundant life. If it brought peace and life, abundance and flourishing, justice and goodness, that was the pasture of God. I've had to deconstruct a lot of garbage about God over my lifetime, but thanks to my mother, I've always known God as abundant life, as goodness, and never as the origin of anything that steals, kills, or destroys us. I know that isn't everyone's story and that many of us were given a damaged and cruel portrait of God. This is something we'll get to in another letter, my friend. However, somewhere along the line, I managed to turn the gift of knowing God as safe pasture into perceiving God as a fortress, missing the reminder that God is also the gate.

For now, be reminded through Scripture and the long, winding stories from the Church, God encounters people in the wilderness. The wilderness isn't always a misstep, sometimes it's right on the map—and when you're in it, you're exactly where you belong. The gate to the wilderness can be a gate to intimacy with God, to transformation, to an encounter with mercy and questions and new friends. God's abundant life isn't found only in pastures and pews; it's also in the cliffs and the wind.

Jesus is our good shepherd on *both* sides of the gate. God is at home where you've been and where you are, and wherever you are going, beloved. There is danger and wildness in God,

---

* John 10:10, MSG.

just as much as calm homecoming. The gate is open because it's time for a wander in good company, even if it's just your own.

THE FOUR STAGES OF FAITH FORMATION

Over the years, I've come across a dozen descriptions of, theories about, and explanations for this deconstruction or faith-shift experience. I'm so grateful for those who go before us to form language for the phenomena of our life. We don't feel quite so alone when someone else articulates a similar experience. I've used a lot of these in my work, from Ricoeur's first naïveté, critical distance, and second naïveté to James Fowler's six stages of faith and Father Richard Rohr's two halves of life and beyond. Lately, the one that's resonated with me the most was developed by Reverend Brian D. McLaren—who, full disclosure, is also a pal. In his book *Faith After Doubt*, Brian synthesized a dozen of these theories concerning faith formation to develop his own four stages, which I think offer a beautiful and accessible path: Simplicity, Complexity, Perplexity, and Harmony. All of these stages are precious and important, even developmentally appropriate.

Simplicity

In Simplicity, we are dualistic and committed to constructing. This is the stage of our life when we rely heavily on black-and-white thinking. We're eager to please authority figures, like our parents or pastors. We highly value loyalty and purity. There is good and there is evil, all is sorted. Sometimes we can be narrow-minded and judgmental, sure, but we're also very committed, and we often are trying to do good in the world. We tend to frame everything in the context of obedience versus disobedience, good versus evil, right versus wrong. Our belonging is secure because we're on the right team with the right answers.

This is pretty much the epitome of the city in the metaphor for the wilderness that I introduced in chapter 1. Your belonging is dependent on your conformity, and faith is an agreed-upon set of beliefs. The forces of shame and fear are used to keep people in line. When folks with this mindset are in power over us, it can be pretty terrifying, because we can feel like we're being dragged into an authoritarian regime in religion or politics and beyond. This stage isn't reserved for conservatives or liberals, or for any viewpoint in between; we can all be dualistic.

Complexity

In Complexity, we become more pragmatic. In this stage we're looking at what *works*. We're focused on achieving our goals. We highly value our emerging freedom and independence, and for us now, it's not so much about good versus evil as it is about winners and losers. Faith is often a means to an end. We look for coaches on deconstruction, teachers on theology, leaders in activism (again, none of this is negative) because we're ready to see change, to win, to change the world, even.

My experiences of doubling down made a lot of sense to me in this stage. I had a goal, I needed to achieve it, even if it was a misguided goal of security, safety, and success. When we're here we're often convinced we know it all. We have answers to every problem that needs to be solved. To be fair, we're enthusiastic, true disciples. We're idealists and eager to embody what we're learning even as we're naïve and overly confident at times.

Perplexity

In Perplexity, we develop a critical or relativistic understanding that enables us to be more honest. We become more aware of our biases and mistakes. We're ready to admit that things aren't always good or right. This is the stage when burning it all down makes a lot of sense to us. Challenging the status quo makes sense, but we can become judgmental, suspicious, elitist, frustrated with old versions of ourselves or those who are at a different stage. We see faith as an obstacle or a weakness at best, if not an actual source and cause of harm. So, we lean into our honesty and critical thinking. We could sum up this stage by saying, *But what about . . .* a lot.

For many of us, Perplexity is almost a relief. It's the first time that we begin to be honest about our own story and the stories in which we have found ourselves. It's the first time we allow ourselves to say the true things out loud—and this is its own form of holiness. It's the fine-tuning of our courage and our first attempt to deconstruct authoritarian structures that often oppress and marginalize, too.

Harmony

In Harmony, we embrace a more integrated or holistic posture that does the work of including and transcending at the same time.[2] In this stage we worry less about good versus evil and more about the greater whole. We recognize that we're all connected and we highly value compassion as well as embodied goodness. Faith becomes a "humble, reverent openness to mystery that expresses itself in non-discriminatory love,"[3] according to McLaren. It takes suffering and loss seriously even as it leans into loving presence and creative wisdom. As McLaren writes, "God is not a destination. Like a river, like a road, God takes us somewhere. For that reason, the authentic experience of communion with God leads into communion with all God's creations. The deeper we go into the love of God, the deeper we are led into all that God loves."[4]

YOU AREN'T ON A STRAIGHT LINE

In my work at Evolving Faith, I was initially surprised by how quickly those of us who were former conservatives or fundamentalists defaulted to a Simplicity version of progressive theology that still painted folks as good versus evil or by how our sense of belonging was dependent on being part of the right group and holding the right opinions still, or by how often we still administered litmus tests with fundamentalist harshness. We had changed beliefs or opinions, but our posture was still one of fundamentalism or simplicity. Eventually, though, people's default to Simplicity stopped surprising me. It turns out that we often need to cycle through these stages over and over again in the wilderness. It's all part of the journey.

I've known people who have stayed in that first stage, of Simplicity, for their entire lives, even as their theology of beliefs changes. I've known people who land in Complexity by the time they're thirteen years old and never really budge. There are people I've known in their twenties who have taught me more about an embodied life of Harmony than anyone else. The point isn't to arrive but to keep going. We're a people on the move. When it's messy, slow, mapless, in fits and starts, starless, and lonely, we keep moving.

*   *   *

IF YOU'RE LIKE ME, YOU might find yourself in several stages of faith on a regular basis. It's rarely a neat-and-tidy experience. We can question what belonging means, even while we find community in a local church. We can be grappling with doubt, even as we're trying to offer answers to our kids. We can practice prayer even if we aren't sure what it means, if anything. And even as we wander, we're carrying with us, tucked right into the corner of our yearnings, the hope that the love of God is more healing, more lovely, more alive than anything we could rationalize or dream up. That love is always kind and patient; it's kind and patient toward you, too. The circles of faith formation are really an invitation to deepening love and wholeness. Your whole life can proclaim an evolution of love.

"Not all who wander are lost," writes J.R.R. Tolkien.[5] You're not lost, you're right where you belong on this wandering path. It might be disorienting, there may be danger, but you're not lost. You're on the right journey. It's just a different path than you were expecting when you were handed a brand of faith and told to cultivate and protect it at all costs. You're becoming someone who is more loving, someone who is healing, who is more acquainted with the fragility and belovedness of us all. The deliverance that's waiting on the other side of the wilderness isn't a tidier, nicer version of you with new and better answers: your deliverance was always going to be more Love.

Wandering with you,
S.

Chapter 3

MAKE YOUR PEACE WITH THIS TRUTH: YOU WILL CHANGE

Dear Growing,

There isn't an easy way to say this to you, so I suppose I'll simply say it. You won't emerge from the wilderness unchanged. You are already changing and you will keep changing, and this is both a relief and terrifying at the same time, I know.

My husband and I often joke that we've been married to at least half a dozen different people over the course of our twenty-four-year marriage: we both keep evolving, keep changing. We've loved each version of each other, each new evolution, but every new version of us has chosen the new version of the other.

One weekend, Brian and I went on a getaway up in the mountains in Whistler, British Columbia, for two nights. We had tucked this little weekend into our calendar precisely because we knew that we would need it after an intense season of work and family demands. So we set it ahead of us as a finish line or reward of sorts and, after dropping the kids with my folks at the appropriate time, we set out. We dubbed it our "recovery weekend" because even though Whistler lends itself to constant activity in beautiful surroundings, we were there for the exact opposite of *doing things*. We needed to recover from all the doing of things we had already been doing. So, we slept in. We read novels. We ordered room service instead of finding fun new restaurants. We went for long walks in beautiful places. We drank our coffee in front of the fireplace and watched the snow fall on the trees. We did not check our email, and we did exactly zero productive things. It was marvelous.

One afternoon we drove down a very bumpy service road to Lillooet Lake. Like many lakes in the area, it's surrounded by mountains with dense forests below the tree line and rocky beaches. In the offseason, you can have the whole shoreline to yourself. I had always wanted to visit, but it was just a bit too far from our home for a day trip with the kids, so we decided to take advantage of our recovery weekend to see it. It was snowy, the clouds were low, and the air was chilly, so when we arrived, we had the shore to ourselves.

Lillooet Lake used to be a bright turquoise color, much like other mountain lakes in western Canada, a remarkable color that is courtesy of the light reflecting off the rock flour from ancient glaciers that feed the lakes.

But back in 2010, the largest landslide in modern Canadian history occurred just up the river from Lillooet Lake, and as a result, its water went from being a clear, bright blue to a muddy shade of brown, overnight. Ten years later, the silt from the landslide was only just beginning to settle. On that late autumn afternoon, the water looked as silvery as a minnow, the expanse stretched out before us. We stood on the shore for a good while, breathing deep in the silence of the wilderness.

As we bounced away from the lake on a backwoods service road, I turned us toward familiar conversations about the possibility of a million changes. I was very much in an urgent turn-our-life-upside-down mood; I tend to have them every five years or so. I kept throwing ideas at Brian: we could sell our house, let's sell every stick of furniture in it. We could move. We could buy an inn within sight of the sea on the east coast.

We could get a dog, a sheep, a goat, maybe a farm? We could homeschool the kids. I think we should get rid of our phones, cancel Netflix, but wait, *The Crown* is coming back for a new season in a few weeks so maybe we'll do that later? I wondered about quitting writing, quitting social media, quitting everything and becoming a florist. (I have very romantic notions of florists, and I have no interest in having those delusions upended.) Maybe I should write a novel? A poem? Maybe if we change everything I'll feel more settled?

Brian dreamed with me, and we had a lot of fun, imagining every different kind of life we could have at this crossroads. But eventually he fell silent, and then he said, "We have had our own landslides these past few years, eh?"

I knew where he was going right away, and he wasn't wrong. The landslides had swept into our lives, from work to church to theology, to parenting our kids and experiencing deep grief and loss and health challenges. I'd argue that most of us have had a landslide recently: a global pandemic, political upheaval, exploding racial tensions, the rise of Christian nationalism, economic uncertainty, all with the impact and fallout of these reckonings.

Time in the wilderness is often characterized by landslides. The divorce. The diagnosis. The job loss. The loved ones convinced of conspiracy theories. And your own devastations: the regrets for things you said and did or were silent in the face of. Then we wonder why everything feels murky and uncertain. We're living in the aftermath of the landslide, and it does take time for the dust to settle.

Brian and I sat in silence for a few rocky minutes, his truck creaking with every dip in the road. "You're saying that we need to let the silt settle," I said slowly. "If the clarity isn't there yet,

I guess the invitation is to wait until something true emerges." We agreed that the aftermath of a landslide—or six—isn't the ideal time for a major life decision.

As we drove back home the next day, every once in a while one of us would start the now-familiar refrain of urgency for change or a drastic upending. The other would respond, "We're letting the silt settle."

MAYBE NOW ISN'T THE TIME for you to upend everything. Maybe now is the time to let the silt settle until things are more clear. Whether it's in your relationships or your beliefs, your vocation or your location, your internal self and your external circumstances—maybe give it a minute. Maybe now is the time for patience and kindness, even toward yourself, your questions, your regrets. Clarity will come when it's time; there is no worry that you'll miss it in the kin-dom* of God. If you're feeling unsure and frustrated, directionless and angry, you can't force a resolution. It's not time until it's time. We are unlearning bad habits, including the need to manipulate and orchestrate a natural process that simply requires time to do the work of clarity.

Maybe we're so used to being in crisis mode, running from fire to fire, from boycott to brouhaha, we have forgotten that we have a life already. Madeleine L'Engle writes, "We've forgotten what it's like to live in a peaceful and reasonable climate. If

---

* I have been using "kin-dom" in place of "kingdom" for a while now, but I first encountered this shift in the work of Dr. Ada Maria Isasi-Diaz's Mujerista theology. Basically, while the word "kingdom" reinforces notions of hierarchy and colonial power, simply dropping the "g" gives breathing room for inclusive solidarity and a mutual sense of kindredness in the concept Jesus taught us and embodied.

there is to be any peace or reason, we have to create it in our own hearts and homes."[1] Yet we live in a time when the absence of peace and reason feels chronic and acute, no matter how earnestly we work for peace.

In times like this, we can either be swept away or we can hold fast, creating the peace and reason and patience we crave while the silt settles. Hold tight to the vision of what you yearn for while the chaos slides down the mountain. Hold tight to the love, joy, peace, patience, kindness, goodness, faithfulness, gentleness, and self-control.[*] The one who has promised is faithful.[†]

Remember, there is still a lake out in the mountains of British Columbia, letting the days pass, the silt slowly settle, the current ebb and flow while the slow, steady accumulation of time brings clarity again. The process is both inside of time and outside of it. It can't be rushed and it can't be managed; it can't be avoided. Slowly, slowly, faithfully, faithfully, the water does the work it is meant to do. And when you can see the sky in the turquoise water again, it seems to me that you'll know everything you need to know, but not a minute sooner.

Isn't that faithfulness, too?

CATCH AND RELEASE

I know a lot of us arrive in the wilderness unwillingly. It isn't entirely our choice or our agency that leads us here. But we often feel a bit defiant and protective, too. We think, *Well, I'm fine with releasing this and that, but this particular thing? That I'll hold on to until the bitter end.* If we think we know what

* Galatians 5:22–23.
† Hebrews 10:23.

we're here to do or learn or become, we will be surprised by the way the wind and waves upend our precious masquerading-as-foundation sandcastles. I'll never stop being surprised by the things I've held on to and the things I've learned to release.

Father Richard Rohr writes, "Most of us were taught that God would love us if and when we change. In fact, God loves you so that you can change. What empowers change, what makes you desirous of change is the experience of love. It is that inherent experience of love that becomes the engine of change."[2] This has proven truest to me in the wilderness. You're being changed and transformed, yes, but it's because of God's love for you and in you and with you. Your faith isn't meant to be unmoved. Be moved.

Open your hands. Release your expectations. Don't try to craft the narrative anymore. Don't erect new guardrails for the swift course of the Spirit in your life. Your faith isn't going to be a dusty antique, held behind glass, a monument to who you used to be. It's dynamic and evolving, changing in fits and starts and mistakes and glory because faith is somehow so human.

I know you have an idea of how this ends: you don't, not really.

I know you have a preference for how this journey unfolds: you will be surprised.

I know you have a long list of things that you can't imagine questioning or changing or releasing: eventually you will.

I know you want some control precisely because you feel so out of control: now you're learning the difference between agency and control.

I know you feel like the old version of you is dying: you're being born again.

BORN AGAIN, AGAIN, AND AGAIN

One night, long ago, an important and well-known man came to visit Jesus. He arrived in the darkness, perhaps because he didn't want anyone to see him or to know about this conversation. Perhaps he simply chose the time when he figured Jesus wouldn't be surrounded by crowds of people and he had a better shot at a good long talk without interruptions. Whatever his motivations, he wanted to know more about this teacher, he wanted to talk to Jesus, and he arrived at night. His name was Nicodemus. The conversation goes like this:

Late one night, [Nicodemus] visited Jesus and said, "Rabbi, we all know you're a teacher straight from God. No one could do all the God-pointing, God-revealing acts you do if God weren't in on it."

Jesus said, "You're absolutely right. Take it from me: Unless a person is born from above, it's not possible to see what I'm pointing to—to God's kingdom."

"How can anyone," said Nicodemus, "be born who has already been born and grown up? You can't re-enter your mother's womb and be born again. What are you saying with this 'born-from-above' talk?"

Jesus said, "You're not listening. Let me say it again. Unless a person submits to this original creation—the 'wind-hovering-over-the-water' creation, the invisible moving the visible, a baptism into a new life—it's not possible to enter God's kingdom. When you look at a baby, it's just that: a body you can look at and touch. But the person who takes shape within is formed by something you can't see and touch—the Spirit—and becomes a living spirit.

"So don't be so surprised when I tell you that you have to be 'born from above'—out of this world, so to speak. You know well enough how the wind blows this way and that. You hear it rustling through the trees, but you have no idea where it comes from or where it's headed next. That's the way it is with everyone 'born from above' by the wind of God, the Spirit of God.'"*

I've always loved that weird phrase "born again." I know it's a little fraught for some, bizarre to others, but I understand it a bit more now, aside from all the baggage. We are born again throughout our lives, becoming new people, starting over with a whole new reality, a new way of being in the world. Sometimes trauma can rebirth us; other times it's revelation or joy or circumstances. It can be obvious or it can be entirely hidden in our souls.

Becoming a mother was one of the most spiritually transformative experiences of my life.† It not only changed my body, it changed my mind and my heart and my soul. Before my first child was born, I never imagined I could have such a capacity for love or for selflessness or patience or prayer, let alone the capacity to fold the amounts of laundry a family of six can produce. Fix it, Jesus.

Becoming a mother has not been a static experience, though. I suppose technically, I was born a mother when my children were physically born, yet I become a mother again and again with less obvious milestones. With each choice, with each meal, with each nighttime sickness, with long conversations,

* John 3:1–8, MSG.
† I don't say that prescriptively—as if every mother shares that experience or ought to!—but it is my own experience.

with tears on the floor in prayer, with arguments. Motherhood for me is the joy and work of a lifetime, too. I come more fully into my identity as a mother in the daily choices of my life to love my children, to honor them, to pray for them, to choose what is best for them instead of what is easy for me. Motherhood is an ever-expanding experience of love for me, and that is transformative, refining.

Yes, I became a mother all those years ago. But I still become a mother every day.

And our children become more themselves every day, living into their own experiences of being born again and again. The first baby I brought home in the mid-2000s is not the same as she was then: as I write this, she's driving my old minivan, bringing home pamphlets for universities, and clocking in for her shift at the grocery store. She is and she isn't still the baby with the triangle-mouth I held in my arms. She's still the kid who dressed up as Darth Vader for Halloween when all the other girls showed up in princess dresses. She's still the kid who read Roald Dahl books under the covers and wrote stories to swap with her friends and tacked up a life-size poster of the human body in her bedroom to more easily memorize the musculoskeletal system in grade three. And she isn't that either. She's who she is now and who she will be, and I will remember and love all the old versions of her even as I love the woman she's becoming. I can't lock her into who she was once, I have to stay in step with all of her evolution to know and love her well as she grows and becomes herself.

That's the thing about a birth. It isn't an ending. It is a beginning and embarking. And I think that's why when we are "born again"—when we begin a new life in Jesus with intention and choice—it is an act of Spirit. It's transformative in a way that transcends formal labels and theological arguments. It's a beginning. There is so much more than we could imagine coming on the other side.

You are being born again, my friend. The old versions of you will be left behind. Sometimes it'll be on purpose, other times it'll surprise you. But one of the kindest things I can do for you is to simply bless your transformation. God is faithful to you in this, too.

Your broken, devastated, tender heart right now is a gift. Look at you, in the midst of your uncertainty and unknowing, embarking on a journey you know will cost you so much, knowing you are saying farewell to the old versions of yourself, and offering this up to the world with hope and love, again and again, anyway. God, it's beautiful.

You can love who you are becoming,
S.

Chapter 4

DON'T BE AFRAID, YOU CAN'T WANDER AWAY FROM GOD'S LOVE

Dear Beloved One,

When he was in elementary school, our son Joe loved contemporary Christian music. Yes, I'm talking about the music on stations with pledge drives, music that promises to be both positive *and* encouraging. He loved it so hard. He knew the words for every song, and if you thought you were tired of "I Can Only Imagine" back in 2005, come back to me after you've listened to it on repeat for an hour.

One day, the whole family was in the car and our eldest daughter, Anne, was in charge of the music. She began to play songs from my high school days, blasting Nirvana and R.E.M. for us to enjoy. I declared Kurt Cobain a Great American Artist. Joe nodded thoughtfully and said, "Just like TobyMac, Mum, you know: the greatest American artist."*

Bless.

Joe and I often took long drives together in those days. He had a medical condition that required us to see a specialist in a city about an hour away several times a year. It wasn't a serious situation, but it was ongoing for much of his young life. There were two perks to Joe's ordeal, however. First, after his appointment, I would buy him a medium pop from McDonald's for the trip home. Second, he was in charge of the radio. That

---

* Currently in high school, Joe has definitely evolved musically and theologically himself since this long-ago day.

meant that several times a year, I also got a medium pop from McDonald's and was then subjected to two solid hours of contemporary Christian music. After a while, resistance was futile and I sang along with abandon at the wheel.

One day, I asked him if he wanted to listen to some of the old-school Christian contemporary artists of my day, just to mix things up. God will forgive me, but I just *couldn't* hear "I Can Only Imagine" even one more time. Joe was game, and so we spent the next hour curating a playlist of DC Talk, Jars of Clay, Caedmon's Call, Burlap to Cashmere, and Waterdeep, among many other artists from the eighties and nineties. He mentioned that Rich Mullins popped up as a suggestion from the app, and I put down my foot: that was it, we were going to listen to Rich Mullins right that minute. No more of this playlist nonsense.

Like most people of my generation who came of age in evangelical-adjacent churches, I was introduced to Rich Mullins through his hit song "Awesome God." I was in junior high when that song was released, and every church in my world played it every single Sunday. I can see my old self right this blessed minute in my memory: standing up in a floral print dress accessorized with choker necklace and Doc Martens, among the modest people in the small churches of my youth, all of us singing our hearts out, over and over *and over*.

When I was in grade ten, I found myself in a relative amount of trouble, and my concerned parents gave me the gift of starting over. At my request, they changed our phone number, co-operated with my cover story that they had forbidden certain friendships, and enrolled me in a school at the complete other end of Calgary, effectively giving me a fresh start. Of course, there is a time when it is wise to make our children walk out a story of redemption in the place of their crashing, but then there are times when our children require a rescue and new ground if they are to ever find their footing. This time for me was the latter.

The main consequence for my mother—other than her relief that I had agreed to go to church youth group again as part of the bargain we had struck—was that she had to drive me to school and back every single day. In the mornings, when my sister got on the school bus, long after my dad had left for work, my mom and I climbed into her teal early nineties Mustang GT with standard transmission and began the trek to the other side of town. She arranged her entire workday around my school bell.

At first those thirty-minute drives felt like a form of torture—not only to me but to my mother as well, I imagine. Over the past few years of turmoil and conflict, my mum and I had lost the ability to speak the same language. Everything I said to her was wrong. Everything she said to me was annoying. We could not find our way to each other and, given the circumstances, silence was preferable to arguing—which may be a chapter title in every parent's memoir about raising a teenager. We drove thirty minutes to school and thirty minutes home in silence every single day, five days a week for at least a month. We couldn't even agree on music, and so the silence continued.

Then came the day when my mum presented a new cassette tape for our consideration: it was Rich Mullins. I had not listened to Christian music in years, and I was so tired of the silence between us that I conceded: *yes, we could listen to this one.* One drive after another, she offered Rich Mullins songs, and one drive after another, I would shrug and say, "Whatever, sure." Then we began to sing along with the tape. We liked the lyrics, we liked the style, and then we began to like each other again. Singing those songs turned into tentative baby steps of conversation. We talked about Rich Mullins, about the songs we liked, and then eventually, slowly, my mother and I began to talk again.

I remember her singing the line from his song "Elijah,"[1] "people have been talking, saying they're worried about my soul" and then glancing a grin at me, eyebrows raised. She knew how church people talked about me. She knew it bothered me, too.

"Let them worry, I know your soul is fine," she said firmly, with more eye contact than the speed limit would indicate reasonable.

Eventually I believed her. I still do.

People will talk, my soul is still fine.

BY THE END OF THE year, we didn't need to listen to music much anymore. As soon as we got in the car, we galloped across the bridge that music had created for us and met in the middle, where we now talked about everything from tests to church, from her own story to mine, from work to boyfriends. The drive felt short now.

When I got my driver's license and an old brown half-ton truck, my sister transferred to my school, and so the drive became the two of us, barreling down the highway twice a day every day, blasting Country 105 like the two Alberta girls we were. We talked and sang and laughed; we were just seventeen and fifteen years old. My mother returned to regular working hours, and she kept the Rich Mullins tape in her console. I used to say that Rich Mullins gave me back my mother, but now I know it is just as much the other way around: his songs also gave my mother back her daughter.

I thought of that as Joe and I drove down the highway together, listening to these old songs so many years later. And when the song "Elijah" came on, I fell silent. Suddenly, I was back in the passenger side of my mother's car singing every line with her . . . I was fifteen years old, learning how to drive a stick with her beside me, clutching the door in fear . . . I was in my old brown truck, driving away from her but always carrying her with me.

Joe sang along while staring out the window, tapping his hand on his jean-clad leg. My eyes welled up and my throat caught at the sight of him next to me. Joe turned toward me and saw the tears on my face. He reached across the divide and held my hand.

"Your soul is just fine," I said out loud when we got to that part in the song, just as my mother had done for me.

"I know it is," he said comfortably.

IT'S OKAY TO BE AFRAID

Are you worried that you're in dangerous territory? Are you worried you're going to go to hell? Are you worried that you're at risk? Are you concerned about the way people are talking, saying they're concerned about your soul? Are you scared? Therapist and writer K.J. Ramsey writes, "Fear is not always a lack of faith, it is a lack of perceived safety."[2]

Most of us have acquired the idea that fear is our number one adversary, or that we need to resist our fears, or even that fear is a liar. We've been admonished, "Do not be anxious for anything,"* as if fear is a moral failing and a spiritual crisis. But fear is pretty normal, even helpful, and if you grew up or were deeply formed by a lot of threats or boundaries and caution based on your right behavior, well, "misbehaving"—doing something other than what others expect—can make you legitimately afraid. There is a fear of judgment, of punishment, of consequences. But fear is simply your body's response to perceived threats. It's just trying to keep you safe, so really, it's an invitation.

"I think that's the kind of wilderness that kicks faith into evolution," said Barbara Brown Taylor at our Evolving Faith conference one year. "You know, one where the death of your identity, the death of your certainty, your old community, your life as you've known it—those deaths are all entirely possible. They're all in mortal danger. And though the dangerous thing doesn't have to kill you, it can. Otherwise, you're not in a wilderness; you're in a park."[3]

Let the record show, I would prefer a park. Few of us would describe the wilderness as a safe haven. But still, God says "fear not," and so rather than simply and only telling you "don't be afraid," I want to invite you to listen to the invitation of your fears. Why are you afraid?

My spiritual director often reminds me, "The kingdom of God is not in trouble." Neither are you. You're not in trouble. Your soul is just fine. Promise. But theology has consequences in our actual lived lives, doesn't it?

My own story of coming to faith was mostly led by love, as

* Philippians 4:6–7 NIV is a wonderful passage of Scripture, but it can be weaponized against us, for sure.

were my deconstruction and renewal. However, I know a lot of us have a different story here—you were, and maybe still are, terrified of hell, scared of God. Scared into your baptism by lakes of fire and devils with pitchforks or those heinous Judgment Day tours at Halloween or "hell houses" at youth groups. You had nightmares. Many of us absorbed that old "sinners in the hands of an angry God" message from the hellfire-and-brimstone revivalist and slave owner Jonathan Edwards, even if we've never read it or heard it, because it has deeply shaped religious life in the West since it was originally preached in 1741. In the infamous sermon Edwards claims, "The God that holds you over the pit of hell, much as one holds a spider or some loathsome insect over the fire, abhors you, and is dreadfully provoked. His wrath towards you burns like fire; he looks upon you as worthy of nothing else but to be cast into the fire. He is of purer eyes than to bear to have you in his sight; you are ten thousand times as abominable in his eyes as the most hateful, venomous serpent is in ours."[4]

Nice, eh? And people wonder why so many of us have religious trauma.

Maybe you desperately tried to "get people saved" because you earnestly desired to snatch people from the jaws of hell. Or you made multiple trips to the altar just to pray The Prayer™ again—and then again—just in case. Every misstep brought crippling fear of offending God and being on the outside again. Belonging depended on conformity, and the box you were given for God could barely hold a thimble of mystery. There was a sense of urgency and fear. Many of you have said to me that you're so afraid of being sent to hell because you don't believe the things you used to believe.

I hate this so much, and I'm sorry if that is part of your own story. Theology has consequences. And those consequences can heal us or hurt us.

Using out-of-context and misunderstood proof texts from the Bible, we were given a vision of a sadistic monster-god, pleased to torture for eternity. Now that's a lie from the pit of hell—and I say that not even believing in a literal hell.* This world has enough horrifying tyrants and torturers and cruel monsters: we don't need to make God into one or try to baptize such things with sacred language. That is truly profane.

AFRAID AND BELOVED

Here is why I'm so convinced you don't need to be afraid of God because you are changing and evolving in your faith: God is love. If there is one conviction I'll carry to my grave it is that God is Love, love, love.† Love looks like many different things, but never once is God's love going to steal, kill, or destroy us. God's love is abundant life.‡ The invitation to the wilderness is an invitation of love.

If we've seen Jesus, we've seen what God is like§—a God who laughs with children, deals tenderly with hurt and hurting people, eats with sex workers and tax collectors, turns water to wine, welcomes home prodigal sons who broke their heart and reaches out to eldest sons who missed the whole point, tells stories, heals, resurrects, weeps, naps, turns over tables, throws open the doors, embodies a message of love and shalom, forgiveness and goodness unto death and beyond.

---

* I say that as a joke, but yeah, I don't. It's fine. We'll talk about that another time maybe. Or not.
† 1 John 4:8
‡ John 10:10.
§ John 14:9.

God showed us through Jesus that no longer will we be servants—indentured, held hostage, or fearful. Instead, God calls us friends.* We are the children of God, made in Their image, beloved.† As John wrote, "This is how God showed his love among us: He sent his one and only Son into the world that we might live through him."‡

Later in that same chapter: "And so we know and rely on the love God has for us. God is love. Whoever lives in love lives in God, and God in them. This is how love is made complete among us so that we will have confidence on the day of judgment: In this world we are like Jesus. There is no fear in love. But perfect love drives out fear, because fear has to do with punishment. The one who fears is not made perfect in love. We love because he first loved us."§

In story after story, Jesus reveals all the ways we've misunderstood and misrepresented God. This is the good news: God loves us and is here to rescue us, not to condemn us.¶ Cast away the old visions of bearded Zeus, of paternalistic punishers, of Bible verses as weapons, of faraway fear coming home to roost, of switches and beatings described as love. Such things aren't love. They never were.

The love of God isn't a far-off destination we are striving to arrive at. Nor is it a prize that will be given to us only if we earn it. It's not for the winners or the ones with answered prayers. It's not just for the ones clutching their pearls over you. It's not just for one denomination or church or religion. No, we are all loved *now*.

* John 15:15.
† Genesis 1:27.
‡ 1 John 4:9.
§ 1 John 4:16–19, NIV.
¶ John 3:16–21.

Here in the wilderness Love will look different than you were taught. It will be tougher and stronger and more stubborn. It will be plainer, healthier. It might look like a kitchen table, not a pew. It might look like enforcing boundaries with people to love yourself well in the midst of this, too. It may look like protesting and organizing, donating money and defending science and offering forgiveness. It might look like conflict and confrontation. Let your imagination about love be set free, imagine even loving yourself well. There are so many ways to love one another once we remember that we are loved already.

YOUR TRUE HOME

The love of God for you is the truest thing in this universe. My friends, it is my absolute core conviction that you are all deeply, completely, and fully loved.

You are loved, you are loved, you are loved. We are loved.

You don't even have to believe it for it to be true. Isn't that nice?

God's love is greater than our worried hearts and their anxious warnings. There is no accusation or condemnation. You can open up your hand and receive what God has already given to you, and then, because you are so beautifully loved, you can, in response, love not only God but one another.

There is this passage in David's Psalm 139 that has been a lot of comfort for me. He writes,

Where can I go from your spirit?
Or where can I flee from your presence?
If I ascend to heaven, you are there;

if I make my bed in Sheol, you are there.
If I take the wings of the morning
and settle at the farthest limits of the sea,
even there your hand shall lead me,
and your right hand shall hold me fast.
If I say, "Surely the darkness shall cover me,
and the light around me become night,"
even the darkness is not dark to you;
the night is as bright as the day,
for darkness is as light to you.*

There isn't anywhere you've been and there isn't anywhere you're going where you're not at home in God's love. The wilderness is home to God, even the wilderness inside you. Your life is already a place where God is quite at home.

God's arms are open wide to you,
S.

* Psalm 139:7–12, NRSV.

Chapter 5

CULTIVATE HOPE ON PURPOSE

Dear Heartsick,

Cultivating hope can feel like foolishness in this economy.

And yet.

And yet.

And yet.

THERE'S A STORY ABOUT AN encounter with Jesus that I find incredibly hopeful even though it looks like the opposite at first glance. It takes place on the third day after Jesus's trial, crucifixion, death, and burial. A small group of grieving women has discovered the empty tomb of Jesus, where an angel tells them that the one they seek has risen from the dead. They immediately rush to inform the other disciples of this wild news, but the book of Luke says that no one believed the women. (Imagine that.) Finally, Peter goes to check it out, and sure enough, he finds the tomb empty. But there are no angels there, and he's left wondering what it means. Shortly after this, we come to the story of the road to Emmaus, where two other disciples have heard the bewildering news that Jesus's tomb is empty. They are on their journey home, talking over everything that has happened. And right in the middle of their conversation, "Jesus himself came up and walked along with them but they were kept from recognizing him. He asked them, 'What are you discussing together as you walk along?' They stood still, their faces downcast. One of them, named Cleopas, asked him, 'Are you the only one visiting Jerusalem who does not know the things that have happened there in these days?'

" 'What things?' he asked.

" 'About Jesus of Nazareth,' they replied. 'He was a prophet, powerful in word and deed before God and all the people. The chief priests and our rulers handed him over to be sentenced to death, and they crucified him; but we had hoped that he was the one who was going to redeem Israel. And what is more, it is the third day since all this took place. In addition, some of our women amazed us. They went to the tomb early this morning but didn't find his body. They came and told us that they had seen a vision of angels, who said he was alive. Then some of our companions went to the tomb and found it just as the women had said, but they did not see Jesus.' "

Jesus then takes the time to explain the Scriptures and everything that has happened. When they arrive at their village, they urge this stranger to stay with them, and it is when he breaks the bread at the table that "their eyes were opened and they recognized him, and he disappeared from their sight. They asked each other, 'Were not our hearts burning within us while he talked with us on the road and opened the Scriptures to us?' " They raced back to Jerusalem to tell all the other disciples their story.*

* Luke 24:13–32 NIV.

WE HAD HOPED

An extraordinary encounter for so many reasons, yes, but did you catch the three heartbreaking words there in that story? "We had hoped."

We had hoped.

These travelers had hopes, and those hopes came to nothing. We don't fully know what they hoped for, but we can guess. Perhaps they hoped that Jesus would redeem Israel. Maybe they were hoping that he would be their great liberator, the Messiah they had longed for. Maybe they were hoping for specific words and mighty deeds for their particular circumstances. Maybe they had hoped for redemption, or for him to overthrow the Romans. Maybe they had hoped that Jesus would somehow talk his way out of this one; he did that sometimes. Perhaps they had hoped the triumphal entry in Jerusalem meant something.

In his commentary on the book of Luke, Justo L. González notes that even the possibility of resurrection isn't enough to wipe away their sadness. "They are disappointed because they expected certain things from Jesus, in fulfillment of the ancient promises made to Israel, but these things had not come about . . . Apparently they are sad not just because Jesus has died but also because he has not met their expectations."[1]

We had hoped.

TO ME, THIS MAY BE the reality of the wilderness that we are experiencing right now. Sure, there is anger. There is grief. There is sorrow and fear. But there is also disappointment, there is our thwarted hope. The product we received did not match the advertisement.

Proverbs tells us that "hope deferred makes the heart sick, but a longing fulfilled is a tree of life."* And perhaps that is what I recognize in those three heartbreaking words, *we had hoped.* It's heartsickness.

When I think about the stories we have brought with us, I can hear that same refrain: *we had hoped.*

We had hoped that the people who introduced us to Jesus wouldn't be deceived by Christian nationalism or conspiracy theories.

We had hoped our marriages would survive.

We had hoped our friendships would last even as we changed.

We had hoped the church would love the LGBTQ+ kids, the immigrants, the widows, the poor, the incarcerated, the disabled.

We had hoped that if we raised our kids a certain way we could guarantee a particular outcome.

We had hoped purity culture would give us a healthy view of sex but, boy, what a nightmare that turned out to be, eh?

We had hoped our lives would look different than they do.

We had hoped our prayers would be answered in that ICU in Nashville.

We had hoped we could bring our whole selves to church.

We had hoped the Gospel would be good news and glad tidings for everyone.

We had hoped for justice.

We had hoped for so many things.

* * *

* Proverbs 13:12 NIV.

MAYBE YOU HAVEN'T EVEN ADMITTED yet that you are heartsick and disappointed.

Maybe Jesus hasn't met your expectations. For what it's worth, I do think it's worthy and good work to interrogate our expectations of Jesus. Sometimes we're like the disciples, who expected one type of Messiah and got the crucified Lamb of God instead. Sometimes our expectations need to be disappointed in order to make room for the true, the wise, and the good realities of God.

But here's the thing about this road you're on: You're here because you still dared to hope.

You took it seriously, didn't you?

You dared to hope the Gospel was true.

You dared to hope that Jesus meant what he said and God is love.

You dared to believe that the Church could be a sanctuary for the wounded and the misfits and the marginalized.

You dared to hope that we are all made in the image of God.

You dared to hope prayer changes things.

You dared to hope you would be loved and that you could love in return.

You dared to hope that Jesus's teachings and way of life would matter more than politics or power, that truth and goodness matter.

You dared to hope for friendship, justice, and belonging, for shalom.

You dared to hope for peace.

In his song about the road to Emmaus, Jason Upton says, "The two fools on the road to Emmaus / They might as well be you and me."[2] We're carrying our heartsickness and our disappointment with us. We've heard of resurrection, but we aren't sure what that even means yet or if we believe it.

And yet—"Were not our hearts burning within us while he talked with us on the road?" we might ask each other later. Maybe.

ON THE DAYS WHEN I believe this,* right on the road, in the middle of our despair, in the dust of our disappointment, perhaps—perhaps—we are walking with Jesus in ways we can't even recognize yet.

And remember that the two disciples weren't afraid to say aloud to this stranger on the road the reality of their situation and feelings. They weren't afraid to admit they were sad. That they were disappointed. That their hopes hadn't come to fruition in the way they expected. They were confused—and they didn't pretend it away or spiritually bypass it either. We can grieve the friends we have lost, the dreams that have died, the ideals that became bitter reality as we well know by now.

We can say, "The women tell me there is resurrection but I'm just not sure what to believe now."

There will be those around us who will say we've walked away from Jesus, but instead, here he is on the road with us and we simply don't always recognize him.

I wonder if there is room in your hope, if not for resurrection yet, then for the companionship and guidance of the Spirit as you travel.

Cultivating hope isn't an empty or naïve thing for you any-

---

* This is a phrase my friend Rachel used to use, and I've adopted it in honor of her, yes, but also because it's true. I don't always believe. So on the days when I do, it's worth noticing.

more. You need to fight for it, you have to contend for it. Because you've suffered and you've grieved. You've had your certainties blown to hell, and it turned out that God was the One who lit the match.

That defiant, scrappy bit of hope you still hold and tend like a campfire in the dead of night tells me you're not done yet. The fact that you're here tells me some little spark, some little pilot light of hope resides in the furnace of you.

YOU HAVE EARNED THIS HOPE

I'm not speaking of the stupidity of silver linings or the violence of "everything happens for a reason" or privileged optimism. I'm not talking about the anemic idea of pretending everything is fine or just being certain "it'll work itself out and anyway, yay for heaven." I see something so different when I look at Christian hope. I see hope that takes suffering and grief and injustice seriously, that takes our liberation and our joy and our flourishing seriously. This isn't a dismissive or pat-on-the-head platitude. We don't live and move and have our being within a Love that denies our full humanity.

You won this hope. You worked for it. You earned it. Your hope deserves your honor and your love.

Your hope turns over tables in the Temple. Your hope is how you vote and march and protest, and as the wise Reverend John Lewis said, "make good trouble." Your hope shows up for the lonely, the needy, the sick, the stranger. Your hope sings songs and sets another plate at the supper table, braids the hair of children and writes poems. Your hope is planting gardens in the very place of your exile.

Your hope isn't an escape hatch or an inoculation against

struggle or a way to avoid being human. This is the hope that has seen a few things. This is Hope with lines on her face and silver in her hair, Hope with strong arms and steady feet rooted and planted in the love of God. Hope with a fist raised in protest, crying out in the streets that Black Lives Matter. Hope showing up, knowing fully well that she will be disappointed again, and even that knowledge doesn't scare her. This is hope that rises each morning and makes the coffee and keeps freaking going.

DON'T SURRENDER YOUR HOPE JUST yet. Don't let them take it from you. Bring it with you even as you travel. Tend it even as you leave behind the toxic beliefs and habits and spaces that do not bring flourishing to you or to the world. Your hope—your hope in the goodness and welcome and love of God, you wonderful, stubborn thing—will not disappoint you. You can take a risk on hope again. A longing fulfilled is a tree of life, and Revelation tells us about that tree of life, that its leaves are for the healing of the nations and the renewal of all things.* We're still walking toward Emmaus. Our hope is with us. And soon, our eyes will be opened to who was walking us home all along.

Even still,
S.

* Revelation 22:2.

Chapter 6

TELL THE TRUTH
AND LEARN TO LAMENT

Dear Heartbroken,

Near the end of my pregnancy with our fourth baby, dreams began to take over my sleep. I've always been a bit of a dreamer, but this was different. The dreams were oddly consuming and consistent in content.

Every night, I would dream in vivid detail of my actual self, in the actual moment. As in, I would be in bed, wearing the exact pajamas I'd slept in. And then I would dream that I was waking up from a dream in my own bed, but waking up to find that I had given birth to the baby in my sleep or was just seconds away from delivery. I would feel an absolute tidal wave of grief and fear and anxiety, followed by a profound sense of aloneness, and then I would wake up. It would take a few panicked minutes before I realized that I was dreaming, that it wasn't really happening.

Every night, multiple times a night, I would have this dream, only to wake up for real and discover it was just a nightmare. Eventually, I began to dread bedtime. I stayed up later and later, hoping that if I was well and truly exhausted, I would sleep without this dream. I never did.

At my next routine appointment, I told our midwife that I hadn't been sleeping well, even beyond the usual restlessness of pregnancy. I was exhausted and sputtering, all because of the dreams. But I told her in the way that I always tell things that alarm me: I joked about it. I have some weird affliction that makes me downplay or deprecate my own fears or needs, which is another bit of baggage to unpack at another time perhaps. I told her about my upsetting dream and its frequency, and then I tried to crack a few jokes at my own expense. I asked for tips to sleep better, chalking my nightmare up to a million excuses: I'm older with this pregnancy, I have three other tinies at home already, I'm working too much, et cetera, et cetera.

Of the many, many reasons why I loved our midwife, one of the most consistent is that she had a very finely tuned bullshit detector. She almost instantly saw right through my aw-shucks and I'm-fine-it's-fine-we're-all-fine posturing to the real story underneath. And so, without missing a beat, without even cracking a diplomatic smile at my attempt to disarm my own fear or worry, our midwife looked me right in the eye and said, "Sarah, have you ever dealt with the trauma from your son's birth?"

And just like that, I couldn't breathe.

IT HAD BEEN SEVEN YEARS since our second baby's, Joseph's, unattended, unintended free birth.* With him, things progressed a lot faster than we anticipated, and long story short, we delivered our son in our apartment building's underground parking garage in front of a crowd of strangers. It's a story I've told a million times, usually for a laugh. I wrote about it on my blog with a breathless urgency and hysteria in the immediate aftermath, then in my first book as an illustration. It became my icebreaker anecdote at women's retreats and my sermon illus-

---

* If you read my book *Jesus Feminist* you may remember that story.

tration when I preached at Christmastime. I had so many good jokes or funny details of that experience, all down pat.

I would tell people about how I hung on to a cement pole and hollered at my husband that the baby was going to *FALL OUT* as he scrambled for our Chevy Trailblazer. I would tell them about the crowd of aghast strangers standing around us, calling 911 on their flip phones. I would crack a joke about how I was so glad that this happened before the days of smartphones; otherwise it would have been all over social media before the placenta was delivered. I would tell them about the guy who walked by in the middle of it all, took in the scene, and said, "Yeah, I think I'm gonna take the bus. . . ." I would tell them about standing up with my husband's arms under my arms while a total stranger knelt at my feet to make sure that the baby didn't hit the cement floor; and how I reached down and delivered that nearly nine-pound baby boy into my own hands.

I always got a laugh when I told everyone how I was whisked away in an ambulance with our son while Brian was left standing alone in the parking lot wondering what in the hell just happened. In shock, he just mechanically started cleaning the floor instead of following us, which gave rise to a lot of teasing at his expense.

Oh, I had *all the jokes* for that birth experience. Hahaha. Ha.

Afterward, my mother would occasionally broach the subject with me, wondering if I was as upset by that experience as she was. But she underestimated my ability to compartmentalize. I can compartmentalize like it's my spiritual gift. I'm even better at compartmentalizing than I am at being passive-aggressive, and *that* is saying something.

* * *

IT DOES FEEL LIKE OUR culture gives out gold stars to people who get over things quickly. We want people to heal on a time line. Yes, yes, that's terrible but *aren't you over it yet?* And like any former evangelical overachiever, I wanted my gold star, my positive and encouraging testimony. So I decided to be fine about the experience. Just fine. Completely over it, able to laugh about it, no big deal.

So seven years later, when our midwife gently asked if my dreams might have something to do with that experience, the familiar instinct to self-deprecate, make jokes, protest that everything was fine in the end was already worn with use. No, I have not dealt with that trauma, Madam Midwife. In fact, I do not feel like I am allowed to be traumatized because it turned out fine. Look! See! A healthy baby! He's a big boy now. Everything is fine! I'm fine! He's fine! We're all fine! Let's move on! It ended well and so let's not make a fuss about it.

But because I refused to acknowledge it in my awake life, I was now reliving that moment of feeling so completely out of control, so afraid, so alone, so unprepared, so exposed, over and over and over again in my dreams. My soul wouldn't let me get away with sanitizing that story, not anymore.

As soon as my midwife paused, her pen in her lap, her eyes straight on me, I knew that she had sliced right through to the issue. I had not reckoned with my fears and trauma from my son's birth. And so my spirit or subconscious or whatever you want to call it was going to keep tapping me resolutely on the shoulder until I finally did so. I didn't need tips on how to sleep better. I needed to deal with the unresolved trauma of that birth.

If we don't deal with our trauma or our sadness or our anger, it begins to deal with us. If we don't allow ourselves to feel our feelings, they have a habit of peeking around the corners of our lives, breaking in at unexpected moments. Trauma or disruption or betrayal manifests differently for each of us—rage, anger, self-harm, self-neglect, frenzy, numbing, posturing, spiritual bypassing . . . Or in that particular instance, nightmares.

OUR ONE COMMON DENOMINATOR

Four years ago, my friend the author and songwriter Amanda Held Opelt experienced a devastating season of loss with the sudden death of her beloved grandmother, followed by multiple miscarriages, and then the very public and unexpected death of her only sister, Rachel Held Evans. In the aftermath, I remember her telling me that her inner landscape and her outer world felt like a town after a tornado had touched down: all of the familiar landmarks were gone. The street signs and lamps had been pulled away and thrown far, the houses of friends destroyed, the map of her life unrecognizable. In this torn reality, you can't find your way to the corner store you visited every week: the roads are gone, the landmarks you used to give directions have disappeared, and even if you manage to get to the right spot, the corner store isn't as it was. You know you're standing in a place you know or knew, but you can't get your bearings because all of the ways you've always navigated your life have been destroyed.

Life may feel like that for you. You're disoriented because everything you knew has been destroyed or it's upside down and flooded. The map is obsolete and you need a new one.

IN MY CONVERSATIONS WITH PEOPLE like us, the one constant thing, the thing we all seem to have in common, is that we've experienced loss. Even if we don't lose our faith or belief altogether, we've experienced loss in relationships, in community, in our own sense of self. I don't know what you've lost so far, but I'm sorry. I also know that even you don't fully know the depth of the losses yet. Part of what we are invited to learn out here in the wilderness is how to metabolize that loss into compassion rather than bitterness, into welcome rather than caution.

My own losses in the wilderness came slowly at first (they often do). Then they began to accumulate. My husband and I lost friendships we thought would endure. We lost the church community where my children were raised. We lost a sense of calling as my husband left full-time vocational ministry. We lost beliefs we once built our whole lives upon. We lost networks of support and professional partnerships. We lost mentors. Definitely lost some innocence. Rose-colored glasses? Long gone. I lost my answers. I lost my sense of direction. I lost so many versions of my own self along the way; as Joan Didion said, "I have already lost touch with a couple of people I used to be."[1]

For many of us, the Covid-19 pandemic is deeply entwined with our experience in the wilderness. The pandemic intensified our collective sense of damage and grief, and it touched every area of our lives. Millions of people died, and the fallout continues to affect everything from housing to healthcare, schools to family dinners. It has been an intense season of loss, grief, pain, and uncertainty the world over.

It makes me wonder how much of our collective trauma or sin or grief we have still not dealt with. The places in our lives where the truth is tapping us on the shoulder, patiently waiting for eye contact. I wonder about purity culture and spiritually abusive churches, celebrity pastors and the damage done in the name of God. I wonder about the toll of soft patriarchy that we call "complementarianism" and dress up with sacred language. I wonder about all the gay kids in church, afraid to come out. I wonder about the pastors' wives who never feel more alone than at church. I wonder about the wounds we carry. I wonder about the reckoning, the apocalypse, as we are simply carrying on, carrying on, even cracking jokes, modeling our resilience, when the whole time, well, somewhere our bodies, our spirits, know it's not quite that simple.

Sometimes we judge or rank our sorrows or wounds; I know I do. I feel I don't get to be sad when other people are sadder for better reasons. I stack my sorrows up against the sufferings of others and think because I don't have it as bad as someone else that I don't get to grieve, I don't get to talk about it, I don't get to deal with it. Just like in my parking-garage-birth story, because I survived that delivery and because Joseph survived that birth experience, *I had to be over it.*

But I was not over it, not really. It had just taken me many years and my literal subconscious sabotaging my sleep to admit it.

How much pressure do you feel to sanitize your story so that it doesn't make people uncomfortable? What anecdotes have you crafted in order to make your struggle acceptable and palatable? Are you laughing so that no one notices your unshed tears?

THE STAGES OF GRIEF ARE NOT A CHECKLIST

When our losses start to accumulate, we often cycle through the stages of grief as identified by Elisabeth Kübler-Ross and David Kessler: denial, anger, bargaining, depression, acceptance.[2] These stages aren't just for grief at the finality of death, they're for the countless losses we can experience as we evolve.

And, as grief always does, it manifests differently for each of us, and we don't know until we know. There isn't anything wrong with this. You're not a bad or a faithless person for the way grief shows up in your life. There is a wandering nature to this grief work. Not everything you do will be healthy and wise, but even that's part of the process. You'll stumble around and make mistakes and be a bit sloppy, no one escapes that part.

The word "stages" can make it sound like a steady climb up a staircase from one to the next, in a linear one-and-done checklist, but that isn't the case. The stages are simply responses, responses to our feelings or our triggers or encounters throughout time. We can start anywhere and cycle through in any fashion, depending on what we're experiencing and encountering.

Most of us were discipled in a faith that relies on steps and formulas and if-this-then-that rules. This is another thing you're losing, I'm afraid. Don't try to make the wilderness into a formula. Don't challenge yourself to complete these steps in a calendar year, despite your track record with yearly devotionals and thirty-day-Bible-reading-plans, eh? As Kübler-Ross and Kessler write, "Our grief is as individual as our lives."[3] You're not meant to hit each stage and check the experience off a list; you're charting a new map of your life by living into it.

Basically, you're not doing it wrong. You can't do this part wrong. But there is no escape hatch, no rolling the dice to skip ahead to Go (and collect $200); you'll visit all of these stages time and again, until they become old friends, good companions, and wise teachers to you.

Denial

Denial can be our insistence that these losses, this wilderness—well, it's not that bad. I'm fine. We're fine. Everything is fine.

I'm not sad. These losses don't hurt. There is numbness to this stage, almost a state of shock. This is often a grace, to be honest, because we're just trying to get from one end of the day to the other, and a bit of denial allows us to set a slower pace for ourselves.

Anger

Anger is a scary one for a lot of us. We feel anger at our old selves, anger for our mistakes, anger at the people who hurt us or left us or traumatized us, anger at the religion or system, anger at the role we played in the systems themselves, anger at our church or partner or friends or politicians, anger at God, anger at the losses, anger at our own self. The anger can feel endless.

We are often discipled in hiding or suppressing anger, rather than feeling it, so when the full force of our anger manifests, yes, it is scary for us and those around us, but that's only because we haven't learned the strength and healing that's possible on the other side of our anger. As author Glennon Doyle writes, "Anger delivers our boundaries to us."[4]

Bargaining

Bargaining is a familiar one to me. I did a lot of bargaining in the early stages of my own deconstructions. I've wondered since then if this is because I came from a tradition that did see God and God's blessings as a transaction: *if I do this thing, God, you do this other thing for me.* So if I pray and memorize Scripture and give tithes, then God will bless me, et cetera. When I first entered the wilderness, bargaining made a lot of sense to me: if I pretend I don't have questions, if I hit all the marks I used to know, surely I can work out a way to be spared from this.

In this stage we find ourselves saying, "I'll never do this again," or "If I can just have back what I've lost." We endure a whole universe of *what if?* and *if only*. I remember being so sure that I could just find a new church, a better church, that would cure my grief and soothe the loss of our community and friendships. I thought that if I kept my mouth shut about my shifting beliefs or the depths of my convictions, I could remain in "fellowship" with others. I thought hiding my anger made me a better lady-Christian.

There can be a deep river of guilt underneath our bargaining. We see all the ways we failed and how, if we could have done things differently, maybe we'd be somewhere else by now. If I had prayed more? If I hadn't read that particular book or blog post? If that person hadn't done this thing, if I hadn't met them at all? Even though some part of us knows better, we feel like we would do anything to mitigate our losses, and so we try making temporary truces with our discomfort.

Depression

Depression is an experience many of us share, and it can last for a while. In this response, we withdraw. We are unbearably sad. We struggle with the ordinary tasks of our life because, well, why bother? We wonder what the point is of going on, of trying at all. But when what you're going through is terribly depressing, it makes sense to be depressed. You are having an appropriate response to something sad or traumatic.* Your sadness is bearing witness to the depth of your love.

---

* There are different types of depression, from postpartum depression to seasonal affective depression to major depressive episodes and beyond. They require different things for different people. Please don't misunderstand me: because the fact that depression is a normal response in grief does not mean you need to deal

Acceptance

Acceptance is one of the more misunderstood stages, I've found. We tend to think of it as a goal, like one day we magically come to be at peace with what has happened in a benevolent transformation. Like, yes, this was terrible and hard and traumatic, but now I'm better. *See, look? I'm so wonderfully okay. I lost a church, now I have a new church. I lost my marriage, now I have a new relationship. I lost my childhood faith, but now I have this other weird new scrawny one I'm nurturing.* But that isn't how it works, is it?

Acceptance isn't a goal, it's an experience you'll have once in a while, and then more often over time. It might not ever feel okay or all right or good entirely. We know better by now. Your losses don't disappear. New friends don't replace old friends. A new church doesn't replace the old church. A new relationship doesn't remove the pain and trauma that accompanied the end of the earlier one or erase the good that was there, too. This isn't a zero-sum swapping game.

But eventually we do learn to live with our loss. We navigate the new normal until it becomes familiar. We rebuild the town destroyed by the tornado, put up old street signs, and maybe add a few new corners and turns. We begin to hope again. We begin to try to reach out again. We find new forms of community. We practice rituals to help us not only with our grieving but also with our growing. We begin to live again on the other side of loss. As poet Naomi Shihab Nye said, "Before you know kindness as the deepest thing inside, / you must know sorrow as the other deepest thing."[5] We share that knowing, don't we?

---

with it alone. Please reach out for help from your doctor or a qualified therapist for support, no matter what form of depression you may be experiencing.

Finding Meaning

Since Kübler-Ross and Kessler's original publication on the stages of grief, David Kessler has devoted his time to the study of *acceptance,* eventually identifying a sixth stage, called Finding Meaning.* When Kessler lost his twenty-one-year-old son, he experienced grief as a father, rather than as a "grief expert." Influenced in part by Viktor Frankl's incredible work,[6] he began to explore how we find meaning in grief. "The meaning is what we do after," he writes. "The meaning is in us. That's where the meaning lies. That's what we can create."[7] This is the work we find out here, too. We are finding, even making, meaning out of what we know, believe, experience, and hope.

FINDING MEANING IN RITUALS

After her own tornado of grief, my friend Amanda Held Opelt went on to explore the traditional rituals of grief and grieving as part of her own journey. She writes,

> The self-help industry has convinced us that we can "life-hack" our way to ease and blessedness. If we are self-care savvy and adequately mindful, then we can circumvent any of life's inconveniences and promptly experience well-being. We are optimizers to the core, absorbing bite-size therapeutic aphorisms via Instagram as we stand in line at the grocery store or wait in traffic. If there's a shortcut available, we'll take it. If there's a speedy solution, we're sold. But there is no life hack for grief.[8]

* With the Kübler-Ross estate's blessing.

Amanda writes so beautifully about twelve historic rituals for grief, like keening, telling the bees, even Decoration Day—all ways that our ancestors embodied and experienced grief, rather than trying to life-hack their way out of it or pretend that it's fine. She writes,

> A ritual is not magic, it simply ushers us into the reality of our own mortality and aids in the acclimation to a significant loss. I picture rituals like smooth stones stretched across a rushing river. They provide the next right step across the torrent and set our bodies in motion. I needed an empty vessel for my grief. I needed time-honored traditions and tested rituals. I needed a next right step.[9]

If you are also needing a "next right step," perhaps this is it. There isn't a life hack for grief, or for the particular grief that accompanies a faith shift like what you're experiencing. However, I've found that the practice of ritual has been helpful to me in that white-hot center of loss.

Finding meaning allows our stages of grief, the depth of our loss, to turn into something that brings flourishing right in the desert. It's the invitation of Jeremiah, encouraging the Israelites to plant gardens in the places of their exile.* Creating rituals and moments of meaning at the crossroads of your loss is a form of healing, too. It's a form of resurrection, right here and now. We will experience a dozen small deaths here, and we'll witness a dozen small resurrections, too.

Some of those deaths and resurrections will be yours alone.

* Jeremiah 29:5 NIV.

As we cope with and metabolize our losses, we'll often need to forgive ourselves for the harm we may have done—on purpose or inadvertently.

We have funerals for death. How about those of us who've experienced the death of our communities, our old selves, our relationships? The lack of ritual can mean we never really feel like we grieved it. In my conversations with people about this, I've been impressed by how many people developed their own little memorials and ceremonies to grieve loss.

In the Evolving Faith online community, we had a Longest Night service on winter solstice. In the midst of the tinsel and relentless cheeriness of the Christmas season, we set aside that night, as many faith communities do, to acknowledge those among us who were grieving or heartbroken or finding the season difficult. With poems and songs, readings and Scripture, we took time as a community to bless this difficult, lonely time. We grieved together. We created little practices of darkness and light to bless both in community and to make room for the grief and our collective processing. It was permission to grieve together, to remember that God is with us even here.

Another friend of mine took a year to write letters to her old evangelical self who was hard on people, yes, but even more severe and unforgiving with her own self. Rather than responding to her former self with frustration, anger, or mockery, she wrote tender little notes telling the old version of herself that she loved her. "I forgive you for what you didn't know yet," she wrote. "I know you made these choices because you were looking for security and love. We are figuring that out now."

After her divorce, another friend wore her wedding dress to the lake and, with a witness or two, went for a swim. Then she shed the dress and emerged from the lake to her friends' cheers and tears.* You can invent your own rituals and observances: host a bonfire to joyously burn a few things, build a cairn of stones, plant a tree to mark the moment properly in your soul.

My beloved friend Kate Bowler says we should just bless the crap out of everything to do with being human.† It's another ritual we can embrace here in the wilderness. It's an act of hospitality and welcome and compassion even in the midst of our grief, loss, and discomfort.

The ritual of blessing, or even just naming, our places of discomfort or pain or loss changes how we see not only ourselves but each other. We can bless marriages in transition and the loss of a rule book for parenting. We can bless a change in vocation and the experience of starting over, not because it feels good—it doesn't—but because it deserves compassion. Developing a ritual of blessing these crossroads is how we find meaning and find each other again. We can bless our longing for communion and the tables where we hope to belong, and all the ways we aren't sure about much these days. We can and should bless our real lives and our real moments and our real neighbors, our real selves—not in spite of our realities but because of them. And we can learn to bless our losses, our discomfort, our longings, our sorrow, too.

---

* Her friends fished the dress out of the lake later and threw it away properly; no one wanted to litter, even for a metaphor.
† Kate Bowler is a dear friend, but her work has also meant a lot to me personally. She says this phrase—"bless the crap out of everything"—often in her podcasts and conversations. You'll also find it in her book *No Cure for Being Human: (And Other Truths I Need to Hear)* (2022), p. 11. To learn more about how this practice works, I'd recommend her two blessing books, cowritten with Jessica Richie, *The Lives We Actually Have* and *Good Enough*.

TELLING THE TRUTH IS PROPHETIC

In a world—and particularly a subculture like evangelicalism—that can run on mutually-agreed-upon half-truths and outright lies, telling the truth is always going to be a prophetic act. For someone like me, with that ingrained theology of pretending that things are fine, it is an actual spiritual discipline to tell the truth, especially to myself.

Back in the city we knew once, it's easier to not tell the truth. There are attempts at silver linings and cheap grace, extolling the virtues of glass-half-full and everything-happens-for-a-reason platitudes to tie a nice bow on everything. In the face of hurt or abuse, the narrative is too often about the need for forgiveness, not justice.

Learning to tell the truth, even about your own life and experiences, is going to be a new practice for you out here in the wilderness. Don't worry, though: God is your midwife, and She has a very finely tuned bullshit detector after all.

Our whole lives can be proclamations of truth. The truth is that we cannot love a God who isn't present precisely when we are sad, scared, worried, anxious, and angry. I want nothing to do with a God who isn't weeping, too. The God of overcomers and victors is also in the gutters with those of us whose hearts have been broken.

Spiritual Bypassing

Coined by psychologist John Selwood in 1984, the term "spiritual bypassing" is defined as the "tendency to try to avoid or prematurely transcend basic human needs, feelings, and developmental tasks."[10] Kate Bowler is the one who introduced me to the term, perhaps because in her work as a historian of the prosperity gospel,* no other term could more accurately describe my people.

To so many of us raised in a particular sort of conservative Christianity, spiritual bypassing was a mark of faith. If we were sad, we said that the joy of the Lord was our strength. If someone hurt us, we claimed forgiveness we didn't yet feel. If someone died, we held a "celebration of life," not a funeral. Our feelings were to be mistrusted, our emotions were possible traps. If we were disappointed, it was our job to get over it quickly. We assigned negative connotations to basic human emotions like sadness or fear or anger.

The only way to begin healing is to acknowledge the wound. Journalist and editor Scott Berinato writes, "We tell ourselves things like, I feel sad, but I shouldn't feel that; other people have it worse. We can—we should—stop at the first feeling. I feel sad. Let me go for five minutes to feel sad. Your work is to feel your sadness and fear and anger whether or not someone else is feeling something. Fighting it doesn't help because your body is producing the feeling."[11]

Stop pretending that your church didn't break your heart. Stop saying it's fine that you were betrayed. Stop excusing bad behavior and cruelty and carelessness. Stop joking about your pain. Stop trying to be unmoved by the news or by tragedy. What you think is the right and faithful response could actually be the thing tearing you apart from the inside. Until you learn to stop spiritually bypassing your actual life with your good humanness, you won't find meaning, let alone healing.

By the way, it's good and holy to seek help. Like, real proper

---

* For this focus in particular, check out her book *Blessed: A History of the American Prosperity Gospel.*

help. Go see a therapist. Talk to your doctor. If one kind of therapy isn't working, try another. If one therapist doesn't understand your unique experience, find another. Finding a licensed, reputable therapist is good and hard work. Try EMDR* and talk therapy, embodiment workshops and group sessions, whatever. Medication can be a miracle. Talk to a psychologist who specializes in religious trauma—there are a lot of online options nowadays, and many therapists offer sliding fee scales.

LEARNING TO LAMENT

The Bible has a beautiful and strong call to lament that we may have ignored or minimized. Claus Westermann, an Old Testament scholar, points out that there are two poles of Hebrew poetry: praise and lament. "They determine the nature of all speaking to God," Westermann says.[12] When we're in the wilderness, without person or structure between us and the wild, good God, these are often the two languages we are able to speak with integrity: praise and lament.

When I was a kid, my sister and I spent a bit of time in canoes, especially when we had a week or two in the summer out near Lake of the Woods in Ontario. Some of my earliest terrible poetry† was born in an old canoe on Woodchuck Bay, watching the sun set as the loons sang over the expanse of water. My sister and I developed a rhythm for paddling that gained ground quickly. It didn't take us long to figure out that if we both paddled on the same side of the canoe, we turned in

---

* Eye movement desensitization and reprocessing.
† I'm a big fan of writing terrible poetry and never showing it to people. I hope more people do it. Not everything has to be amazing and perfect to be just what you need. Write more terrible poetry!

circles. We had to paddle on opposite sides of the canoe, I in the back on the starboard side, she in the front on the port side. Only with both of us working together on opposite sides were we able to glide so easily through the water in the direction of our choice.

To someone growing up in a religious tradition like mine, it can feel like everybody's paddling on the same side of the canoe, going in circles, getting dizzy, moving nowhere, churning water with no purpose. This is perhaps why endless praise choruses eventually feel empty. It's only when we paddle with both praise and lament that we begin to move forward.

But as Dr. Soong-Chan Rah writes,

> Lament is not simply the presentation of a list of complaints, nor merely the expression of sadness over difficult circumstances. Lament in the Bible is a liturgical response to the reality of suffering and engages God in the context of pain and trouble. The hope of lament is that God would respond to human suffering that is wholeheartedly communicated through lament. Unfortunately, lament is often missing from the narrative of the American church.[13]

It's also missing for all of us who have been shaped and formed by the American church's reach and dominance in our spiritual histories over the decades.

During a season of deep grief and loss, my spiritual director invited me into a small practice of honoring these experiences and emotions. At her invitation, I found an empty jam jar in our pantry, filled it with tap water, and set it on my desk. Beside it, I placed a small pile of salt in a dish along with a teaspoon. Each time I felt sadness, rather than distracting myself or pretending to be fine or whatever trick I wanted to pull to numb or avoid the feelings, she told me to drop some of the salt into the water. In this way, I would actively embody the truth that God holds our tears. It seemed kind of silly to me, but hey, I'm nothing if not game. (This is perhaps the benefit of growing up charismatic, you learn to never discount any possibility of an encounter with God, even in the unexpected places.)

OVER THE NEXT SEASON, I had a lot of reasons to add salt to that jar.

. . . I canceled all future speaking engagements as my health took a bad turn and I couldn't travel anymore, losing years of income, yes, but also an aspect of my vocation. I spooned a bit of salt into the water.

. . . After a season of quiet campaigning about us, we lost our church because of our family's stance on LGBTQ+ inclusion in the church. And I poured more salt into the water.

. . . Another Black man was executed at a routine traffic stop. And I poured more salt into the water.

. . . My beloved friend's son lost his battle with mental illness, and I stood at the edges of her consuming grief. And I poured so much salt into the water.

. . . Lockdowns began. I spooned more salt into the water.

. . . One of our kids ate lunch alone at school every day for a year. I poured more salt into the water.

. . . I sat by the hospital bed of a beloved friend, holding her as the machines were quietly shut off at the end of everything. And when I came home, I poured salt into the water, day after day after day, for months.

Slowly, slowly, I began to learn to feel my grief instead of stuff it down or hide it away or reason with it. I simply let the salt swirl into the water and allowed the jar to hold it all. Each grain of salt reminded me of what the Psalmist wrote, "You keep track of all my sorrows. You have collected all my tears in your bottle. You have recorded each one in your book."* It's a form of soul care to embody that hope that God is with us, still, in the heartbreak of our lives, too.

Lament isn't limited to our personal heartbreaks. Its potential power is unlocked in the community of the suffering. We need lament to remember our story within the story. We need communal lament for gun violence, for murdered and missing Indigenous women and girls, for pandemics, for famines and war, for abuse scandals and cover-ups, for everything lost in this world. For us to have a shot at peacemaking in this world, we need this sort of authentic encounter with suffering, even if it makes those around us uncomfortable.

It will, by the way, make people very uncomfortable.

Lament interrupts our tendency to move too quickly, skipping over suffering, finding too-easy answers that gloss over complexity and pain. Lament clears the path for the fullness of God's love in our heartbreak, not settling for be-blessed-and-highly-favored chirping. Learning to integrate our hope with our lament is the work of the Gospel, too.

A POSSIBILITY OF HEALING

My midwife took the time that long-ago day to walk me through my memories: the sad and scary ones. In the aftermath

---

* Psalm 56:8 NLT.

of being honest with her, we developed plans to empower me, to resolve the trauma, and to walk paths of healing. She entered into deep work with me to prepare for birth again, but also to carry forward into the future. I learned to honestly own the whole story now, the dark and the light of it, and I do genuinely feel healed in body and mind. But it still hurts. It just hurts like the collarbone I broke when I was six: when the wind is right, it aches, but a lot of the time I carry on without being acutely aware of it.

That afternoon, I left the midwife's office feeling lighter than I had in months, maybe years. And that night, I went to bed and I slept. I slept like I hadn't slept in months, easily and dreamlessly.

I believe we can heal. I believe you can heal. Beloved, do you have room for this possibility? You have a possibility of healing, even if everything that was broken still aches when the wind is right. Your experience will come to mean something compassionate and connective to you. The grief might stain the good memories or positive things from before for you, too, but it also changes how you move forward. You'll never forget how it feels to be left behind or left out, cast away or abandoned. You'll never forget how it feels after the tornado. And so already a new map of goodness is being drawn in you. Healing is hard work, harder than we ever knew, plainer and more ordinarily steady than we expect. But what was meant to shame you or silence you or punish you will become the making of you.

Eventually you will learn, as most of us do someday, that just as grief stained backwards over, you'll regain the good again.

Our hearts will always bear the marks of our losses. It's just that one day—sooner than you expect but later than you hope—the stitches that bound up the wounds, the scars you'll carry forever, become deeply beautiful to you, too, as beautiful as the worn hands of a beloved elder and jam jars with salt water only you understand, the patina on an ancient bell in a tower and the deep rest of old places under canopies of faithful trees.

Your story of faith has both darkness and light, joy and sorrow. It may take some time, telling the truth, bearing witness, practicing lament, and finding a ritual or two to mark the moment. You'll always acknowledge what you've lost; don't ever pretend it didn't hurt as much as it did. But you'll learn to have fun again, learn to trust again. As you practice rituals and find meaning, you'll remember the good times as well as the bad.

You'll remember how to sing old songs in crowds of people and develop an instinct for who else in the room is lonely. You'll regain your agency. You'll learn who you can trust, and that will come to include yourself. It may ache when the wind is right, but you'll move with ease within your own story. You might find a new community, you'll rediscover parts of yourself you thought you'd lost.

You'll learn to love your broken heart, each stitch of mending will be there on purpose, and it will be a whole new map of love in your life. It will lead you home.

You're allowed to be sad,
S.

Chapter 7

NOTICE YOUR OWN
SACRAMENTAL LIFE

Dear Seeker,

One cold evening near the end of winter, my two youngest daughters asked if we could go and see if the park's skating paths were still open. Here in Canada, if we went outside only when it was warm and pleasant, we wouldn't leave the house from October to April, so we get very good at bundling up and saying things like "There is no bad weather, just bad clothes!" which isn't at all annoying by late February. At many of our local parks, the municipal governments will ensure public rinks and pathways are iced up so that we can skate on the cheap. Skating at night in parks or on ponds is just one of the ways of our people. Usually there is a firepit or two where folks can warm up. Somehow you never feel the cold quite as acutely when you're young. It's only when you're in the warmth of a pine skate shack with a wood-burning stove in the corner, lifting your frozen feet out of your skates to slip them into the blessed relief of winter boots, that you realize you are actually frozen solid.

That night, the older kids were busy with schoolwork and basketball practice, Brian was at a late work function, and so I loaded up my girls' skates, located the helmets, and got our gear on. I can't skate anymore myself, but I'm good at tagging along. On the way, I warned them that because of the recent blessed thaw, the rink and paths might be closed. They were still game to try, but sure enough, when we got to the pitch-dark park, the ice was soupy from the unseasonable warmth earlier that day. Disappointed at first, we elected to take a walk, since we were already bundled up and we had the park to ourselves.

At the time, Maggie was just six years old, and at first she was nervous in the darkness. Usually it's summertime when we're outside at that hour, and we have our own friendly campfire. This cold nightfall surrounded by giant spruces felt almost alien to her. We held mittened hands as we walked until she realized what we all realize eventually in the dark: when we stop fighting the darkness, it welcomes us as old friends. There is actually plenty of light, it's simply reflected from the moon and the snow. It's a quieter, more subtle light, but it's there nevertheless. Maggie's eyes adjusted and her steps became more certain.

The girls were captivated by the stars, spread across the sky like a banquet. Older kids love to teach younger kids, whether the younger kids like it or not, but Evie has always had a worshipful audience in her younger sister Maggie. She stopped and crouched low, wrapping one arm around her younger sister, the other mittened hand gesturing up to the sky as she tried to point out the Big Dipper and the North Star. "Their light happened millions of years ago," Evie said, waving upward, "but we get to see it still."

"Wow," Maggie whispered, her face tipped up.

Is there anything better than when a kid whispers "wow" under their breath? It sounds like prayer.

They fell silent, gazing up with their winter toque pom-

poms tipped back. Suddenly a star streaked across the sky in a blaze, gone as suddenly as it had appeared. They both gasped at the marvelous sight.

"Sometimes you need a biologist, and sometimes you need a poet," writes Rob Bell. "Sometimes you need a scientist and sometimes you need a song." I would only add, "And sometimes you need a kid." Every walk with a kid invites a slower pace through the wonder of this ordinary life, noticing things like dogs, trees, flowers, rocks, big trucks. It's hard not to feel wonder when the person you're with is constantly amazed.*[1]

DO YOU EVER HAVE THESE moments? When it's just an ordinary, tiring day, and then something streaks across your field of attention that seems precious and important and fleeting all at the same time? Like your brain or your heart or maybe the Holy Spirit stops you to say, "Hey, you're going to want to notice this, trust me." It's the holiest of interruptions.

These are the moments that are saving my life right now.† As Blaise Pascal wrote, "In difficult times, carry something beautiful in your heart."[2] When the world is struggling or when we are exhausted, we are invited to the holy conversation of noticing. Noticing the sanctuaries of spruces still available to us, noticing the stars, noticing our children, noticing the night. We live into the night until it becomes a friend.

---

* I mean, all I want is for someone to look at me the way a baby looks at a ceiling fan, right?

† This phrase originated for me in a Barbara Brown Taylor book. She writes about a "wise old priest" who asked her to speak at his church by telling her, "Come tell us what is saving your life now." *An Altar in the World: A Geography of Faith* (New York: HarperOne, 2010), p. xv.

WONDER AGAIN

Life can be pretty ordinary and domestic. There are teeth to be brushed, appointments to make and keep, phone calls to avoid (just me?), children to feed, laundry to fold, washrooms to scrub, emails to return, bills to pay, time cards to punch in. Church can also feel like another domestic routine, nothing more than a series of meetings, programs, studies, gatherings, pray-this, read-that, think-this-never-that. We become bored or dispirited, even in our souls.

On top of that, along comes a pandemic and the rise of fascism and gun violence, along comes your discontent, along comes revelation of secrets long hidden, along comes your kid coming out, along comes your sense that there has to be more than just routines and never rocking the boat.

Then? Then we realize that we can't survive on safe routines and pleasant boredom any more than we can survive on rage and fear. We need active goodness and wonder and joy, we crave laughter and sleep and good food.

This is your invitation to wonder again.

That's where you are now, you know.

The smallest, and most common, aspects of our lives contain whole worlds. Your burgeoning sense of astonishment is admitting that being useful isn't everything. There has to be room for what is beautiful, simply for its own sake.

"I cannot turn on the writing art or transcendence like a faucet," writes poet Luci Shaw. "My job is to wait and see— literally to wait for the Spirit, with the Spirit, and to see. In this waiting time, I must be sure that my antennae are out, combing the air, ready to pull in the messages."[3] The wilderness is an invitation to unfurl your own antennae again. We may not all be poets, but we all have the ability to comb the air for what we may see of the Spirit out here.

I have a hunch that you're realizing right now that what you need is a steady reclamation of wonder, a discipline of being amazed. You're tired of just eavesdropping on holy conversations, you're ready to chime in.

And yet religion in our modern era seems mostly concerned with systematizing theology, charting time lines, answering questions, and making God small and knowable. We have created a God we can regulate, a faith that fits into the little box we've constructed and mislabeled "Abundant Life." So much of our study of theology has become just a way to stop conversation rather than open it up.

There are a lot of weird stories we've tamed over the years: floods and rainbows, burning bushes that are not consumed, healings, prophets, talking donkeys, fish with money in their mouths and widows with inexhaustible oil to sell, the dead rising. Sometimes I imagine Jesus was awed by the dark beauty of the storm on the water even as he walked upon the waves to his friends, who were afraid. The number of weird and wondrous happenings in the Bible is staggering. But we've removed wonder to turn God into a manageable deity, a force understandable to our minds and our methods and concerns. We're all seeking to tame the wonder because not-knowing is scary to us.

Allowing yourself to finally ask the questions you've denied your own soul is an act of love. There is uncelebrated humility in admitting that we don't know.

Steer into the things that leave you asking questions instead of memorizing answers. See the hand of God beckoning in the invitation of your life. Don't give in to the pressure to domesticate the wild, unknowable possibilities of God and this world and your own soul.

It is my hope that the wilderness will restore your capacity for wonder. It's my hope that you'll relearn how to ask questions and you'll be startled by ladybugs and the return of a robin will make you glad. It's my hope that children and elders will find you a patient presence. And it's my hope that you'll realize that being useful and having answers isn't everything. There has to be room for nonsensical, wasteful, and sacramental noticing, because through it you begin to witness God's heavy pour of love into your cup.

It might sound odd at this stage of your journey to tell you this, but here it is: cultivating curiosity, wonder, and beauty will serve you well in your evolving faith. Honor your doubts and questions, sure, but it's the yearning for certainty that will hold you back longer than you imagine. The insistence on solvable equations and never-ending industry will suck the life out of you just as much as sorting everything into good versus evil, right versus wrong categories. Make room for fascination and amazement; they heal something in our minds and hearts. They even reopen the old doors we sealed shut with religious certainty and boundary markers. It turns out there is a whole world waiting outside.

LET "I DON'T KNOW" BE YOUR ANSWER

My friend Rachel Held Evans taught me to say, "I don't know," and enjoy it. She wrote, "Unfortunately, saying 'I don't know' has fallen out of vogue in Christian circles, and I'm still trying to get used to saying it myself . . . Most of the people I've encountered are looking not for a religion to answer all their questions but for a community of faith in which they can feel safe asking them."[4] If nothing else, the wilderness will give you sacred permission to say "I don't know" more often.

If you've spent a season or even a lifetime shutting down questions and doubt, this is your opportunity to lean all the way into what makes you wonderful and weird. This is your chance to bless every question and then let yourself live into the answers over time.[5]

Saying "I don't know" more often opens up the space that false certainty used to occupy. This is your path to find things to marvel over, from snow falling in the light of streetlamps to the brushstrokes of a painting.

Author Katherine May calls this awakening to wonder *enchantment*. She writes,

> Enchantment is small wonder magnified through meaning, fascination caught in the web of fable and memory . . . It is the sense that we are joined together in one continuous thread of existence with the elements constituting this earth, and that there is a potency trapped in this interconnection, a tingle on the border of our perception."[6]

Our attention performs this miracle, the miracle of reenchanting our days and places. I hope you learn how to say, "I don't know, but isn't it amazing?" more often.

LET GOD SURPRISE YOU

These days, my own knowing of God's love rarely happens in the places where I was told to look for God: church services, quiet times, Christian lady books, worship music, whatever. Don't misunderstand me, if you still find life and goodness in those things, then please carry on. But these days, I feel God's nearness most in the dark, in the public pool, around the dinner table, on unremarkable sidewalks during a daily walk, under a cover of stars. I feel God's love for all of us in sad songs, in lines of poetry, and in the long line of people snaking down the shopping mall aisles, all waiting to pick up a packet of information so they can shop for a local family in need and drop off Christmas toys for kids they'll never meet. It's usually in the homeliest of places and most commonplace moments that I can feel God's love the nearest these days.

RUMORS OF THE REAL

When I was in university, back in the days of VCRs and repeated viewings of *Titanic* at the dollar theater, I had a poster of one of the paintings in Claude Monet's famous Impressionist series *Water Lilies* on my dorm room wall. A friend had given it to me when she graduated the year before, certain her post-university life had no room for posters sticky-tacked in place, creating permanent grease stains on cinder-block walls. I hung it up in my dorm room even though Monet wasn't my personal favorite—I was more of a van Gogh kind of gal— because I thought the poster classed the place up with my stacks of textbooks bearing USED SAVES stickers on the spines and my Windows/286 computer taking up my entire side of the desk I shared with my roommate.

I didn't grow up around people who thought much about art. We were a practical bunch, focused on a good job with a pension and looking forward to Saturdays for *Hockey Night in*

Canada. I didn't know a single person who had traveled to Europe or who went to a museum for fun; that simply wasn't our world. We read paperback westerns and almanacs and the *Regina Leader-Post.* We hung family pictures, maybe the occasional print of horses or a grain elevator, framed embroidery samplers from our grandmothers. We found these things beautiful (I still do, witness the painting of a grain elevator at sunset in my living room this blessed moment).

It wasn't until I entered university and took the required classes in the humanities that I began to learn about art history and the progression of creativity in our world. The classroom introduced me to Picasso and Rembrandt, Rodin and da Vinci, Munch and O'Keeffe. But the problem with a liberal arts education is that you soon learn enough to finally understand just how much *you don't know* about many, many things.

Through all of this, I remained content with my poster of the great painting. Others joined it over the years—postcards of van Gogh's *Starry Night* or Renoir's dreamy *In the Meadow* (which reminded me of my sister and me in the summer) or Klimt's *The Kiss,* pretty typical university student choices. These prints and posters were sufficient for me: the beauty of a reproduction was enough for me.

A couple decades later, however, I found myself in New York City for the first (and to date, only) time. I had flown in early for a speaking engagement, and I had one full day in that famously busy city to spend just how I wanted. It was unforeseen riches to this busy mother of four. I hardly knew what to do with myself.

I landed at 9:00 A.M. and, after dropping my carry-on at the hotel in Chelsea, took a cab to the Upper West Side. Listen, everything I know about New York City is courtesy of Nora

Ephron movies, and so if Kathleen Kelly from *You've Got Mail* lived on the Upper West Side, well, guess where I was going? That's right. I went to Zabar's for a legit bagel with a coffee. And I had one ticket for a matinee of *Wicked* (alas, the brand-new *Hamilton* was way above my pay grade), but I had a few hours before curtain, so I walked my way to and through Central Park, heading for the Metropolitan Museum of Art. Because why not?

The Met was so much bigger than I expected. I walked up the long and wide stairs to the front doors, where I paid my admission, picked up an offered map, and went up the grand staircase in the front hall. I wandered without ambition, finding myself first in medieval paintings and tapestries, walking through galleries of dark religious icons. I kept texting my sister to say some variation of "I wish you were here—you would not BELIEVE this place!" which I'm sure blessed her as she cut crusts off the grilled cheese sandwiches for her daughters on a rainy day back home.

Eventually I wandered through an open doorway into the next gallery. There were tour groups bunched around certain paintings, inspecting them closely; they included an elementary school class who were sprawled on the floor with pads of paper and pencil crayons, copying—oh, good gracious—an *actual* van Gogh painting. Many van Gogh paintings, in fact.

Astonished, I paused at *Wheat Field with Cypresses,* and as I looked at it, the unmitigated reality of it overwhelmed me. When I had seen the pictures in my textbooks or displayed in calendars (van Gogh twelve-month calendar, 1994), I had liked them. I had nodded in agreement when professors or experts assured me of their brilliance. I thought I appreciated them as I learned about the artist and their context. I could identify them if I saw them on note cards I used to send dutiful thank-you notes for Christmas presents.

But then I saw the real thing. The tall, narrow cypresses above the golden field of wheat, all set against a swirling blue sky and mountains. It wasn't just the beauty of this piece itself, it was the realization that every brushstroke was so deeply human. The painting wasn't flat, as rendered in a book; it was textured and alive, each curve of color and blob of paint was an insistent reminder of the realities of life, and even death. Someone painted this, it didn't just arrive out of nowhere, and here in this room, more than a hundred years later, it was still real.

I had heard rumors that the real things were astonishing, but they were just that—rumors. All of my knowledge fell away in that instance of *knowing*: sure, here's a time line and here are the influences and here are the patrons and the historical context and cheap posters, but somehow those rolled to the corners of the room like end-of-season Christmas ornaments because what really mattered was the reality. It was art.

Rumors of the real are a good start. But if this was where my story had ended, I would have missed this moment.

I stood in the museum and I cried.

I dropped my purchase at my feet and I wept with joy at the sight of it. My smile began to hurt my face and I shook my head in disbelief, opening and closing my teary eyes to keep checking that this was all here and all still real.

Look at it, it's so beautiful. It's really real. Van Gogh did this work and here it is and here I am and it's really real. It was a submersion into a new world, as if the room was breathing with life. I wasn't prepared for it. But now I understood: the reproductions were just rumors. They weren't the real thing. They were pale copies compared to reality.

I called my husband and my sister and my mother one after another on my walk back down Fifth Avenue. I cried as I told my girlfriends on Voxer about what I had seen with my own two eyes. I posted pictures on Instagram. I could not shut up about how brilliant reality was in comparison to the rumors of it.

I DON'T REALLY KNOW ANYMORE what happens when we die. I don't know what's waiting for us, if anything. I do have hopes. I have hunches. I have stories. I have ideas, and theology experts tell me all sorts of contradictory things. Perhaps someday we will simply be before Jesus the way I stood before van Gogh's paintings in that gallery. Maybe we will be overwhelmed with beautiful reality, tears falling down our faces, all arguments and time lines and histories and opinions and theologies cast down to roll away to the corners because of their insufficiency to fully understand and touch the clarity of God; the inbreaking of the light. The sight of the Real is when we fully and finally realize just how insufficient the rumors of this Love have been.

There has always been a conversation with God happening, right under the surface of our certainties and dogmas and scripts. In Paul's first letter to the Corinthians, he tells them that we see through a glass darkly. It's right at the end of the well-known "love passage"* often read at weddings, "Love is patient and kind," et cetera. After that, he writes that someday all of our important and even inspired words will end, our prayers will end, our knowledge will end, but love will be what lasts forever.

* 1 Corinthians 13.

* * *

WHEN WE LOOK UPON THE world with curiosity and wonder again, perhaps we're simply picking up a conversation we half remember from our childhoods. We've seen whispers of love, rumors of peace, inbreakings of holiness, flashes of revelation. Near the end of that letter to the Corinthians, Paul writes, "For right now, until that completeness, we have three things to do to lead us toward that consummation: Trust steadily in God, hope unswervingly, love extravagantly. And the best of the three is love. Go after a life of love as if your life depended on it—because it does."*

We build our homemade altars right in the rubble of nonsense and tragedy to bless what remains good, here, right now. Noticing the breath in your lungs, the cold, the cadence of Psalms in your bones even still, the creak of snow under your boots, the prospect ahead of a cuppa tea and a hand to hold. I still believe God is putting all things right. I still believe so many of us are trying to join in that work, and so it is worth noticing what is already steadily ordinarily glorious.

I like how author N. T. Wright puts it,

What you do in the present—by painting, preaching,
singing, sewing, praying, teaching, building hospitals,
digging wells, campaigning for justice, writing poems,
caring for the needy, loving your neighbour as
yourself—will last into God's future. These activities are
not simply ways of making the present life a little less
beastly, a little more bearable, until the day when we

---

* 1 Corinthians 13:13–14:1 MSG.

leave it behind altogether . . . They are part of what we may call building for God's kingdom.[7]

This is why noticing can also be a form of prayer and of praise and even of worship again. It's a conversation with God, in which we say, *Yes, I see the sanctuaries and altars and invitations of this place, these people, this moment, and I won't miss it.* It is precious and important and fleeting, as vital as water tumbling over rocks and coyotes trotting through fields and piles of books. Pausing to notice and name, especially when we are sad or discouraged, tired or overwhelmed, is as good as hallelujah. It's a practice for the wilderness.

WHEN THEY WERE YOUNGER, OUR kids liked to sleep outside on summer nights. Sometimes we set up the little tent in the backyard, but usually, they just laid out their sleeping bags and mats on the deck. One night, when our older three were just about nine, seven, and five, we dragged their camping gear to the deck again, made snacks, and they stayed up too late, giggling and chatting to themselves. Eventually they fell asleep and Brian and I went to bed, our window open right beside them to easily hear and respond. At about two in the morning, I woke up to the sound of their little voices. It took me a minute to realize that they were whispering to one another to wake up. "Wake up, Joey, wake up," Anne was whispering. Evelynn wasn't far behind. I got up and went to check on them from the kitchen door, but when I peeked through the window, I stopped myself from stepping out onto the deck, reluctant to interrupt their own moment together. Their small faces were awake in their sleeping bags, and they were all staring at the sky. I looked up, too, following their gaze, and the stars were spread above them in a great feast of constellations. Have you ever seen stars like this? Not a stingy one in the cosmos, they were a fortune of openhanded light, a riot of fire in the darkness as the earth spun. The kids were quietly awed, and one whispered, "I can't believe we always sleep through this."

Notice the wonder in your life,
S.

Chapter 8

GO SLOWLY ON PURPOSE

Dear Straggler,

Do you remember Exam Day back when you were in school? (My apologies if I've already conjured up your most common nightmare.) There was always a kid or three in the class who thought the point of the test was to finish first; maybe it was you. The teacher would lay the papers on the desks, and on her word, all the papers would be flipped over and the test begun. Inevitably at one point she would say, "It isn't a race. Take your time." But somewhere in the front row there was a small trail of smoke from a busy pencil as someone burned through each question as quickly as possible, rushing to be done.

This usually happens only when we're young, new to test taking perhaps. Once the papers are marked and handed around, the unfortunate speedy one is sheepish over sloppy mistakes, we hear quiet whispers of "I did know that one, I did." We learn that, despite the competitive nature of our cultures and the desire for a winner, it's better to be thoughtful and use all of the time allotted, to ensure that you are understanding and are responding well.

It's not a perfect metaphor, but it's the one that often comes to mind when I see folks out here trying to speed-walk through the wilderness, desperately grabbing answers and filling in the blank spaces with whatever is easy or quick rather than what is right. Perhaps this is because we've been given the anxieties of getting things right and quickly; perhaps it's simply uncomfortable for us to sit with a blank page for a while, let alone to sit with the truth.

I get it. I mean, when I was first beginning to rethink a lot of what I had been taught as a kid in church, I thought I could solve my problems with new theology. And theology isn't just the study of God and God's way of being in the world, it's also what we think, know, study, believe, and perhaps even hope about God. It shows up in our daily, walking-around lives. Most of our choices and opinions can track their way back to what we believe about God, and so, if you believe that God is a strict disciplinarian, angry and impatient and exacting, ready to send you and everyone to hell for a misstep or mistake, then yes, you get that test done efficiently and quickly and under great stress.

But what if God isn't a strict teacher with a ruler and a snide look on her face? What if God isn't a test proctor? What if you could get a few things wrong and still know the friendship and love of God?

Hasn't that been true for most of your life? When you look back over the life that brought you here, have you ever been wrong? Have you ever made a mistake? Have you ever learned new information and then adjusted accordingly? Of course you have. That's because this is how you are human, this is how you are growing up; why would your spiritual life be any different? God loved you then and God still loves you now.

It's this in-between time, when we're not who we were and not yet who we think we're becoming, that can break us. Everything feels a bit more fragile when we leave some spaces blank. When we say, "I don't know yet," it can feel like an admission of weakness or ignorance at first. It's actually wisdom. You're learning to let things settle, to let some answers emerge over time and other questions fade away. Maybe it will serve you well to deep-dive into atonement theories, sure, but maybe what you really need to learn is how to practice loving kindness and the gift of time.

We can be desperate for clarity in the wilderness. The world feels upset and scary, overwhelming, tragic even. We will try to force new answers and radical life changes, believing that if we upend our lives, somehow that will make the uncertainty seem less consuming.

This is your time to slow down, my friend. You've been moving very fast for a long time, trying desperately to get all the answers right. It has felt urgent. And yet this is the slower path, a more homemade path, and there are no shortcuts, no rewards for being done first. You don't have to have it all figured out right now; I know you want to, though. Alas, there isn't a fast pass version of the wilderness. There isn't an app for bypassing the deep, slow work of the Spirit in you and through you.

Tortoise for the win,
S.

Chapter 9

RECLAIM REPENTANCE

Dear Regretful,

You're going to need to reconcile what you know now with what you didn't know before. You will need to practice a lot of patience and kindness toward yourself, offering your own story a bit of the grace you have learned to render to others. You're going to need to make peace with your sins and regrets, yes, but eventually you'll forgive yourself. And part of that process will be turning toward the work of repentance now, relearning how to confess and repent, over and over again.

I've grappled with using the word "sin" in this conversation because of its attendant baggage. Those of us who have the habit of turning over the rocks of religion to see what's underneath are well acquainted with the messy underbelly squirming in that word. But I find I still need it. I need the weight and gravity of the word, the seriousness. Because the wilderness does eventually require us to acknowledge the gap between what we hoped for ourselves and our actual behavior and corporate realities. Pointing the finger at all the ways everyone else around us needs to repent can feel cathartic until we find ourselves squarely in that same realization: that we have our own work to do, that we have our own reckoning with our lives at hand, too. We have our own sin and our communal sins to deal with now.

This may be some of your deepest, most uncelebrated work.

It's the practice most of us want to skip past with excuses and justifications. And we do have them, I know. Some of them are even legit: *You didn't know better. This was normal in your world. No one ever taught you or told you. You were trying your best. You got some things right, you know.* See? We could do this all day. But that doesn't lead to transformation in us or in our collective story. It just maintains the status quo.

It can be hard to talk about repentance and confession. For some of us, those ideas have been a steady and beautiful rhythm of faith formation, but for most of us, not so much. We've experienced manipulation and guilt, gaslighting and shame. We've had repentance and confession weaponized against us, used to control or silence. Others see repentance as a ritual, much like a kid being told to apologize to a sibling when they don't really feel it at all: "sorry if you were hurt," we mumble, while everyone knows good and well that we aren't really sorry, we're just saying what we're told to say in an empty formality.

So for some of us, the word "repentance" initially feels inadequate and passive, like it's just another word for "sad feelings" or "being caught out." When faced with the real-world damage and toll of sexism, homophobia, cruelty, white supremacy, well, the wobbly notion of repentance that contents itself with "I feel bad and I feel sad so let's move on" is woefully inadequate, if not sinful altogether. An apology and a sad-face emoji are skimpy fare when we are hungry for justice.

REPENT

When I hear the word "repent," I am always reminded of that thunder in the desert, John the Baptist. Out in the wilderness, he receives a message from God and then begins to preach, preparing for God's arrival. When crowds of people show up because it's popular to do so, he loses it:

"Brood of snakes! What do you think you're doing slithering down here to the river? Do you think a little water on your snakeskins is going to deflect God's judgment? It's your *life* that must change, not your skin. And don't think you can pull rank by claiming Abraham as 'father.' Being a child of Abraham is neither here nor there—children of Abraham are a dime a dozen. God can make children from stones if he wants. What counts is your life. Is it green and blossoming? Because if it's deadwood, it goes on the fire."

The crowd asked him, "Then what are we supposed to do?"

"If you have two coats, give one away," he said. "Do the same with your food."

Tax men also came to be baptized and said, "Teacher, what should we do?"

He told them, "No more shakedowns—collect only what is required by law."

Soldiers asked him, "And what should we do?"

He told them, "No harassment, no blackmail—and be content with your rations."

The interest of the people by now was building. They were all beginning to wonder, "Could this John be the Messiah?"

But John intervened: "I'm baptizing you here in the river. The main character in this drama, to whom I'm a mere stagehand, will ignite the kingdom life, a fire, the Holy Spirit within you, changing you from the inside out. He's going to clean house—make a clean sweep of your lives.'"*

* Luke 3:1–17 MSG.

*   *   *

JOHN'S WORDS HERE ARE ACTUALLY a lot closer to what we're going for than most of the shame-based, guilt-ridden, empty, even manipulative experiences of a practice like repentance some of us were raised with. We each bring something different to how we understand that word.

Repentance is actually a beautiful, life-giving reorientation toward God's good path of flourishing with ourselves, our neighbors, and our world.

THE CHANGING OF A LIFE

The word that our Bibles usually translate as "repentance" is the Greek word *metanoia*. Etymologically, sure, you can begin to discern what this means,* but even our linguistic work is insufficient for what was meant by the word within the text and within the early Church's understanding of what repentance actually meant for a life and a community.

Metanoia is the changing of a mind that leads to the changing of a life. It is not a mere shift in belief or thought from disinterest but a complete turning away and turning toward that which brings life and flourishing to you and to the world. It's not simply confessing our sins or understanding something on an intellectual level, or feeling convicted—all good things, mind you—it's literally *changing your mind and then changing*

---

* Word nerds, I see you. As *Mounce's Complete Expository Dictionary* tells us, though, "The words themselves are derived from meta ('after') plus nous ('mind, understanding') for the noun or noeō ('to perceive, understand') for the verb. However, the meaning of the words in the NT [New Testament] does not reflect this etymology; that is, metanoeō does not simply mean 'to perceive afterwards'."

your life in response. The word "metanoia" is often used when speaking of life-upending change, like conversion. It's a re-orientation of ourselves toward God and one another. It's the reimagining of the world from the posture of transformation.

This view of repentance is a generous one. It reminds us that, at the core, sin is a turning away from Love. Repentance is turning back toward that path of Love, which is what we're hoping for out here anyway, isn't it?

And that work isn't a one-and-done sort of deal. We are always invited to the continual reorientation to Love. Metanoia abounds in our shared stories, from Mary Magdalene's redemption to Peter's prophetic embrace of Gentiles (talk about embodying repentance and reconciliation!) to Zaccheus's encounter with Jesus. That sort of reorientation—that embodied holy transformation—has implications for our relationships with ourselves, with one another, with the land, with our communities, with our world.

Hallelujah. And uh-oh for the status quo.

Now we know that repentance isn't just cerebral or emotional, it's also embodied. Repentance has weight and heft, sings songs and experiences touch, writes legislation and enacts policy. Yes, it speaks words—because words matter—but it also has action.*

Repentance done right is an embodied atonement. It's not just our confession and forgiveness or even accountability. Dr. Chanequa Walker-Barnes writes, "Repentance . . . is not a one time event involving expressions of apology and forgiveness. It

---

* Notice what's missing from this list? Shame. Hey, beloved. It's true. There isn't shame in repentance. There is conviction, though, the sort of conviction that invites you into the realities of being a person and the possibilities of repentance.

is the gateway to moral repair and to new life, that is, the gate-way to conversion."[1]

When we repent, we are answering the call to reconciliation and transformation that our prophet in the wilderness fiercely delivered. Like Isaiah, John the Baptist is a poet and a prophet, but the kind that hauls you to the entrance of the wilderness and boots you through the gate and tells you, Begin again. *Begin again,* over and over, keep reorienting to God's good path. Be about the work of the kin-dom and the action of grace.

John isn't content with niceties and conventions or hypo-theticals as we read in his invitations to the crowd, the tax col-lectors, the soldiers—he wants us in on the kin-dom and changing direction in our real, right-now lived lives. This sort of repentance has implications for how we show up in the world.

REGRET AND GRIEF OVER OUR sin and our old selves is part of the wilderness package, I'm afraid. We can't undo the harm we have done, purposely or inadvertently. We can't erase the things we said or the sermons we preached, the choices we made or the ways we spent our money. We can't erase the person we were when we were earnest and sincere and utterly wrong. We are reckoning with the realities of our privileges and our mis-takes and our ignorance. There was so much we didn't know and even more that we refused to understand, isn't there?

Maybe this is the beginning of the call for us then, to a re-pentance that is active and embodied. It's an invitation to face a new direction. Without guilt, without shame, without empty words. To simply turn your face toward Jesus, toward the light, toward the peaceful kin-dom prophesied by Isaiah and join God in the work of raising up those valleys, lowering the mountains and hills, making rough ground level and rugged places plain.* Turn toward the vision of shalom and wholeness that promises not one thing in God's universe isn't beloved or is out of reach of redemption.†

OPEN YOUR GRIEF, QUIET YOUR CONSCIENCE

It would be incomplete for us to talk about embodying repentance without talking about reconciliation and even reparations.‡ That's because, if we're doing it right, repentance will lead us to reconciliation. Dr. Brenda Salter McNeil defines reconciliation as "an ongoing spiritual process involving forgiveness, repentance, and justice that restores broken relationships and systems to reflect God's original intention for all creation to flourish."[2] If we have come face-to-face with our sin and wrongdoing, with our complicity and brokenness, then we are invited to enter into a *process* of repentance, not a singular event of repenting. It's a practice of restoration and justice, shalom and peacemaking.

That's where something like confession can become important to us. I know that we're a bit unfamiliar with such a thing in our era of never-apologize and never-let-them-see-you-sweat, but confession unburdens us, frees us from carrying the weight of wrongdoing on our own. The hope is that we will be

---

* Isaiah 40.
† Isaiah 40:4.
‡ Talking intelligently about reparations is above my pay grade (as is most everything I do, but still, even I know my limits). For further reading on this topic, check out *Reparations: A Christian Call for Repentance and Repair* by Duke L. Kwon and Gregory Thompson (Brazos Press, 2021).

met, at the apex of our failures, with prayer and with love. We acknowledge out loud that we screwed up and that we need each other to heal.

This may be one of the reasons that Alcoholics Anonymous and other recovery groups are among the most real forms of community folks experience in a lifetime: they're the safe place to be honest, to struggle, and to admit imperfection, a sanctuary of sincerity, even. We are all in the same boat of failure and longing and even sin; let's stop pretending otherwise. Confession creates the room for the truth to set us free because it invites someone into our realities with us.

Confession doesn't even necessarily have to do with wrongdoing: we can confess that we are tired, that we are confused, that we are weary. Confession is truth-telling. Confession is opening a stuck-fast door to the sweeping-in wind of the Spirit and even the possibilities of forgiveness, the kind that lifts the curtains and freshens the whole house.

The invitation before you is one to more shalom, more peace, more hope, more love, more trust, more wholeness. It's never about shame or power or excuses. In the 1662 version of the Book of Common Prayer, the priest's exhortation before communion reads:

If there be any of you, who by this means cannot quiet his own conscience herein, but requireth further comfort or counsel; let him come to me, or to some other discreet and learned Minister of God's Word, and open his grief; that by the ministry of God's holy Word he may receive the benefit of absolution, together with ghostly counsel and advice, to the quieting of his conscience, and avoiding of all scruple and doubtfulness.[3]

"Open[ing] your grief" and "quieting your conscience" might be a beautiful and practical pathway here in the wilderness. Perhaps we begin with simply opening our grief, cracking open the longing and sadness and absences within us. It's less about how or why or when but simply a matter of inviting someone trusted and proven into the grief caused by your wrongdoing, your cruelties, your pettiness, your unwitting complicity. Repentance is simply opening our grief over the ways we know we're destroying our connection with God, with ourselves, with one another. What destroys us is personal, yes, but it's always communal, which is why things like repentance and confession have usually had a communal call to them: we are not alone.

It is remarkable how much energy is required to ignore or pretend away our failings and weaknesses, sure, but also our longings and desires—those needs demanding satisfaction or acknowledgment that we went about the wrong way. I rarely meet truly evil folks; there is almost always what pastor and author Nadia Bolz-Weber often calls "the thing under the thing" when it comes to what we do wrong or the ways we mistreat each other or ourselves. Perhaps that quieting of our conscience happens when we name to one another the mysterious, hidden parts of us, the ways we have coped and numbed and weaponized our grief and longing.

The roots of our sin are often complicated, deeply tangled in our fears and our desires, our origin stories and context, and our own participation. Sin can be systemic and cultural, it can be embedded in our governments and manifest in our foreign policies. But just because it has a complicated root and we understand why it's there doesn't mean Jesus doesn't want to pull that thing out and set us free from it altogether.

We confess and we hear each other's confessions, we forgive and we are forgiven. We are empowered and beloved at the moment of our vulnerability. We open our grief to one another (choose wisely) and hear the truth our souls long to hear: you are forgiven, go and sin no more, I'm here with you, let's untangle you together. There is no place you can go where you will outrun God's love and longing for your wholeness.

IN THIS PROCESS OF REPENTANCE and confession, you're going to have to learn to allow yourself to say,

Yes, I have done things wrong.

Yes, I am tired of faking fine and avoiding accountability.

Yes, I am weary of being strong.

Yes, I am in need of help.

Yes, I have hurt people—intentionally and unintentionally—and I need to make it right.

Yes, I taught or expressed theology that I deeply disagree with now.

Yes, there were consequences for the things I said and did in the lives of other people.

Yes, I used tactics like bullying or silencing or ostracizing.

Yes, I judged and gossiped and accused.

Yes, the way I act on social media or at work or in my family isn't consistent with my deep hopes.

Yes, I am ready to admit that I get things wrong, that I benefit from systems, that I choose violence, that I am led by my legitimate desires for belonging or respect or love into behaviors that delegitimize others or myself.

Yes, I am complicit with systems of abuse or supremacy or marginalization.

Yes, I am entangled, and I do not know how to get free.

Yes, I have been carrying the weight of this alone, and, God, I'm so so so tired.

Forgive me.

Forgive me.

Forgive me.

WE STOP PLAYING A CARNIVAL shell game with our realities and instead, turn over everything to the light of day, come what may, put it all on the table. I cannot recommend more strongly that you find a companion—a qualified companion—like a therapist or spiritual director to walk this path with you. Because it may feel like this kind of honesty will destroy you long before it has a chance to heal you. But opening your grief to another in this way is actually the path of healing itself, it is also the Gospel.

Healing doesn't come because we're so good at faking fine. In my experience, healing has most often felt like a quieting. This sort of healing comes when we open our grief to one another and practice receiving forgiveness, embodying reconciliation, and turning toward repentance. Healing will require the challenge of transformation. Austin Channing Brown writes that "for most confessions, this is as simple as asking, 'So what are you going to do differently?' The question lifts the weight off my shoulders and forces the person to move forward, resisting the easy comfort of having spoken the confession. The person could, of course, dissolve into excuses, but at that point the weight of that decision belongs to them, not to me."[4]

It would be nice if the resurrection meant that all of this was just poof! over and done with. But instead we are loved by a

God who wants our participation, a communal God who pulls up a chair to our table and says, "Let's get to work together, this is going to be amazing." Gentle and relentless, this is the path we are on.

Practice speaking kindly and patiently toward your own process and becoming, dearest. Repent, confess, be transformed by the embodiment of both. There isn't a race to tidy new answers; sometimes you're going to live into your new realities, and you need to learn some things before you're ready to answer, "What will you do differently now?"

Turning around,
S.

Chapter 10

LEARN TO LOVE THE WORLD AGAIN

Dear Beloved,

A few years ago, I took my children to the edge of the lake in the mountains on another day of snowfall. It was an iron-gray day, alternating between rain and snow right at the freezing point. We threw rocks into the cold water just for the satisfaction of a splash. There was a dead duck at the shoreline, and the kids marveled over it in fascinated revulsion before moving on. The clouds reclined on the hillside. Just that morning, I had been reading poet Maggie Smith and so thought of her line "I'm desperate for you to love the world because I brought you here"[1] as we stood at the edge of the water, my kids' laughter and joy at the fresh air rising after days cooped up inside. Maggie Smith's words became my heartbeat prayer for them: *love this world, love this world, please love it here.*

Perhaps part of what ails us now is that we've forgotten how to love the world. Not just each other in the broad and general sense but this *actual* world, the ground upon which we stand, the place where we lay our heads, the people whom we see right before us.

In his letter to the Ephesians, Paul writes,

Watch what God does, and then you do it, like children who learn proper behavior from their parents. Mostly what God does is love you. Keep company with him and learn a life of love. Observe how Christ loved us. His love was not cautious but extravagant. He didn't love in order to get something from us but to give everything of himself to us. Love like that.*

Watch what God does, eh? And here is what I do know about what God does: God so loves the world.

GOD LOVES THE WORLD, EVERY blade of grass, every grunt and squeal of creatures, every kid who goes to sleep worried about something, every burning bush, every lullaby that we sing. All of it, all of us, held in that extravagant sacrificial love. *Mostly what God does is love you.* Keep company with God and learn a life of love. Learn what a gift it is to be here, alive in your life.

The call to learn to love the world again is a call to engage with all of those Big Things, of course—love never makes us smaller and narrower and lonelier, it never shuts us off and away from longing and hunger. But I wonder what it would be like to love the world again *so much* that we are unable to ignore climate change because the world is crying out for us to love her again. What would it be like to love the world so much that we believe women and protect children? What would it be like to love the world so much that we see the image of God in one another across aisles and streets and po-litical divides and borders and the ones we have been taught to fear and resent?

What would it look like to remember how to love the world again even knowing it will break your heart?

* Ephesians 5:1–2 MSG.

Loving is a worthwhile risk, a shot in the dark that illuminates everything, a radical act of faith and hope. Even in this we are invited to be in step with the God who consents to having Their heart broken and yet runs extravagantly into this world. *For God so loved the world, for God so loved the world, for God so loved the world.*

People love to quote John 3:16—including me, I quoted it just above here—but I've also become partial to the next verse: "For God did not send his Son into the world to condemn the world, but to save the world through him."*

For God *so loved* this broken, longing, beautiful, terrified, burning, glorious, spinning world. We have been brought here for love by love for love in love. Maybe God is desperate for us to love it, too.

THE PRACTICE OF LOVE

I promised to tell you the things that have served me well in the wilderness. This one might surprise you after the last couple of chapters, but it's so important to me now.

I think you should make it your mission to devote yourself to nourishing love in your life.

I think you deserve it. It can be so lonely out here, fearful even. You may not know much, you may be doubting everything you once felt certain of, and you may end up somewhere you never intended or expected.

Somewhere along the way, you may have picked up the idea that love is a gift some people are given and others are denied. You may have developed a starved version of love, dependent

* John 3:17 NIV.

on conditions and with tight boundaries, but it turns out that love is simply a practice you can work like a baker works yeast into bread, right into your life.

I've always liked the word "practices." Perhaps it's because I'm burned out on the old terminology of "spiritual disciplines." Perhaps it's because so much of my spiritual life before the wilderness was an on-and-off switch; you were either "on fire" or lukewarm, you were either healed or sick, you were either faithful or faithless. There wasn't much room for the real muddy work of being a person with contradictions and nuance. Calling something a "practice" implies that you're not good at it yet but you're improving. Practice implies that you're being taught, you're open to correction, you're learning by repetition and challenge. It's one part habit and one part effort with a bit of magic there, too. That's been my experience for a lot of the goodness I want to plant and nurture in my life.

Embracing practices is not a matter of faking it until you make it, it's just a matter of doing something, over and over because you're creating something beautiful with your life. And wherever this path leads you, you'll be grateful for all the little campfires of belonging you found along the way, all the moments of hope you cherished, the brief flickers of love that caught and in the end, became the hearth of your life, warming you right through.

As author K.J. Ramsey writes, "It's as though our choices can bushwhack a path into the wilderness of a new way of being, and the repetition of those choices and habits clears the land into a trail. Eventually, repetition of practices and habits paves the path, so that we can walk down it even when our feet hurt or there's heavy fog blocking the way. Every day, we are learning to trust we know our way back home. With repetition

over months and years and a lifetime, habits of choosing connection, love, and joy can become nearly automatic."[2]

LOVE IN PARTICULAR

Remembering how to love the world while still in the midst
of our own evolution is complicated. We don't need a reso-
lute beam of positive thinking and encouraging chirps about
silver linings. Those sentiments—a cotton candy theology of
survival—melted long ago. You know this. You have likely
learned it the hard way.

But what would it be like to love the world not in general
but *in particular*? Pay attention, be mindful of loving *this particular world* and *your particular people* and *your particular place*
and *your particular self*. Love is not cautious but extravagant
and specific.

I've found—entirely by accident—that the practice of loving *this in particular* a few times a day is actually functioning as
both an invocation and a benediction. Learning to love *this* in
particular—whatever *this* means in that moment—invites the
presence of God (or at least my awareness of it) and blesses as
sacred where God already dwells. This has been a nice surprise.
And so I've landed here right now: remembering to *love this in
particular*.

Love the pencil crayons and markers always on the kitchen
table. Love the curl of steam from the tea in the morning, love
the light in the late afternoon illuminating the crumbs on the
floor as holy. Love underlined poems and the sight of birds on
the wind. Love the noise of the streets and the bass line in that
one song, you know it. Love the donate button on a food bank
website and the satisfying click of finding some small way to

keep loving your neighbors. Love your body, every curve and change. Love the sound of the words "I love you," "I forgive you," "I'm sorry," "I miss you," "I choose you," "I made coffee and it's ready." Love the bark of the big old tree you watch through every season of change.

Love this moment of particular grace, not in spite of all the grief and loss surrounding us but because of it. Love this because now you know that Frederick Buechner was right: this is the world, beautiful and terrible things will happen. Don't be afraid.[3] Beautiful things are happening and terrible things are happening, both are true. Don't be afraid.

Are you remembering to find something, in particular, to love even during this wandering season? There is so much to love, especially out here, right here.

Love something in particular,

S.

Chapter 11

NURTURE YOUR OWN BELONGING

Dear Misfit,

It's almost impossible to talk about belonging without acknowledging where many of us have experienced belonging and exclusion in equal measure at times: church.

I don't know what your relationship is with the church—your particular communities of faith, yes, but also the larger, wider Church. I can venture a good guess that it's best marked as "it's complicated." Me, too, pal. I mean, back in 2015, I published a book called *Out of Sorts: Making Peace with an Evolving Faith*, and it has a chapter that explores my own experiences over the years. It culminates in the story of how I was reclaiming my relationship with the Church universal, but also with a particular congregation for our particular family in our particular place. I hadn't gone to church consistently—or purposefully—in about six years prior to that. Oh, I popped in now and then for Christmas pageants for the then-tinies. I haunted a back row or two and dedicated our two eldest kids at a church that tried to meet us where we were at. But in my heart I was just done. I honestly did not think I would ever return to institutional religion. It wasn't because I had stopped loving Jesus, but I just didn't see a path for loving Jesus and loving people with the expressions of church I knew at the time.

But then, miracle of miracles, we found ourselves in a small church that met in a school gym and I fell head over heels in love. We were there for eight years. In my book, I wrote, "I have learned to love the Church perhaps because the Church has so beautifully loved me. I love the Church in all the places I find her now—cathedrals and living rooms, monasteries and megachurches, school gymnasiums and warehouses." That's still true. I do love the Church. It just turned out that I loved them more than they loved me, perhaps. Like so many of you here in the wilderness, we lost our church and so much of our belonging as we kept evolving.

The church that changed my mind about organized religion, the church where my son was baptized, where my daughters were dedicated, where they all toddler-danced at the altar with flags in hand, where I (not really) jokingly referred to us as "lifers," where I first began to preach on a regular basis, where I nursed my babies in the school classrooms with other mums, ultimately became a place of exile. Our family affirmed and welcomed LGBTQ+ believers into the life of Christ as embodied in life and ministry, and because of that, a line was drawn and we stood on the other side of it. I don't regret this in the slightest, I'd choose it again and sooner and probably better knowing what I know now. It was awkward, intense, complicated, and human. No one was the bad guy, not really, but well, I felt like my heart was broken, and this experience also left its mark on my children, which is always the hardest part.

Perhaps you relate? Maybe you've had your heart broken when a place of belonging became a place of alienation, too. That's the thing about belonging, it can feel so precarious and conditional. We almost all have a story here, don't we? I've heard from a lot of folks over the years, people who feel that they didn't so much "leave" their church as were left by their church.

Many of us don't feel safe in church; we never did, because of our questions or convictions, our identity or social location. And after we've had our heart broken, we often wonder if God is okay with us taking a break from church or maybe giving up on the idea altogether. We've experienced beauty and ugliness in those communities, and that matters. It's important to name, acknowledge, and even bless our complicated, unfinished stories.

Some of us around this campfire have lost or been kicked out of or abandoned by or stormed from churches. Some of us have been or are pastors right this blessed minute, often aware that if we were honest about our questions, doubts, or evolution we'd be out of a job. Some of us have experienced nothing but love and care and community within churches. Others have found gossip, drama, shallow relationships, culty behaviors, and even abuse. Some of us didn't just lose a church, we lost a whole community, all of our friends, or even our vocation.

MAYBE IT'S STILL A GROUP PROJECT

The early Church referred to itself as *ekklesia*. From the preposition *ek*, which means "out of," and the verb *kaleo*, which means "to call," the word literally means "the called out ones." The word also shows up in the Greek Septuagint to refer to Israel as an assembly of the Lord or a congregation.[1] It describes a range of encounters, everything from a meeting to a battle. The early Church defined herself as a people called out, now gathered by Jesus, and connected to the old, old story God began with Israel.[2] The Church is simply the people of God gathered in community. Ideally, this means that we reflect God's love, not only toward and with one another but within this world God so loves. We're meant to be a foretaste of the kin-dom of God, a tangible signpost on what the First Nations Version of the New Testament refers to as "Creator's good road." We are called to embody an alternative to the world's way of doing things, the world's way of being in everything from our worship to our social order to our work. We're called to embody God's redemptive goodness in the world, together.

Did you catch that word "ideally" there? Because yes, we long to be—and often are—the "gathered and sent" community of our highest aspirations, called to care for each other and build each other up.* Not only through formal programs but in our informal way of life. In that good way of being, we see mutuality, forgiveness, someone to laugh with and to cry with, people who will pray for one another, mutually meet the needs of one another both materially and spiritually. Ekklesia is meant to be a source of belonging.

But sometimes there can be a mighty big gap between our ideas and our reality. We often have a real yearning to idealize the early Church, but most of Paul's letters—and so our New Testament—exist because of all the ways the early Church was wilding out and not living up to those ideals as well. The one consistent thing in the Church through the ages is messy people. So perhaps it shouldn't come as a surprise that the Church nowadays continues to balance precariously between our ideals and our realities as a place of embodied community.

---

* Ephesians 4 is a lovely treatise on unity in the Church, especially verses 1 through 6, which in the NIV read, "I urge you to live a life worthy of the calling you have received. Be completely humble and gentle; be patient, bearing with one another in love. Make every effort to keep the unity of the Spirit through the bond of peace. There is one body and one Spirit, just as you were called to one hope when you were called; one Lord, one faith, one baptism; one God and Father of all, who is over all and through all and in all." *happy sigh*

After being stung a time or two, the understandable temptation is to simply go it alone. To isolate. To avoid each other. But as bell hooks writes,

> We have to beware of the extent to which liberal individualism has actually been an assault on community. The notion that "real freedom" is about not being interdependent, when the genuine staff of life is our interdependency, is our capacity to feel both with and for ourselves and other people.[3]

I think that interdependency is something we're all craving, even if it will look different from how we were taught to value it.

When my friends Rachel, Jim, and I started Evolving Faith, we envisioned a one-and-done retreat weekend, but when actual people showed up, they made it incredibly clear to us: we need ongoing community. It became the number one request from the people who hung out at the conference: is there a way we can stay in conversation and community, even beyond this? We eventually launched a little online community to make an attempt in that direction. The wilderness can be so deeply, profoundly lonely, can't it? And finding some form of community along these pathless hills matters, even if it's just for a brief moment in time. As author and podcaster Katherine May said,

> More and more, I crave being part of a congregation, a group of people with whom I can gather to reflect and contemplate, to hear the ways that others have solved this puzzling problem of existence. Most of all, I want them to hold me to account, to keep on track, to urge me towards doing good. Holding spiritual beliefs on my

own is lonely. I want to be part of a group that makes me return to ideas that bewilder and challenge me.[4]

EXPAND YOUR PRACTICE OF BELONGING

So, I wonder if you could expand your practice of belonging? It can include a more formal church congregation, of course, but it isn't limited to that. This will sound like a gotcha! from a former youth pastor, but it is still true that we don't *go* to church, we *are* the Church. No one gets to take Jesus away from you and no one gets to disqualify you from the Church. It is Jesus's table, none of us are in charge of the guest list, we're just the happy, rowdy ones squishing over to make more room. The fact that a particular church congregation has rejected you does not mean God has rejected you. Historian and theologian Diana Butler Bass writes,

> If we think of belonging only as membership in a club, organization, or church, we miss the point. Belonging is the risk to move beyond the world we know, to venture out on pilgrimage, to accept exile. And it is the risk of being with companions on that journey, God, a spouse, friends, children, mentors, teachers, people who came from the same place we did, people who came from entirely different places, saints and sinners of all sorts, those known to us and those unknown, our secret longings, questions, and fears.[5]

This understanding runs contrary to how a lot of us were raised: with church on Sunday morning, Sunday evening,

Wednesday nights, youth group, programs, camps, "building the house" as the central axis around which all of the rest of your life turned, all meant to bring us to Jesus and to each other and to the world. And that's fine . . . right up until it isn't.

Your sense of belonging isn't dependent on that. I think I always knew this in my heart, but it really came home to me during the years when I traveled a lot to preach. For a few years there, it felt like I was preaching almost every weekend all over Canada, the United States, and even in the U.K., as well as at my own scrappy home church. I was honored to worship with Episcopalians, Baptists, Pentecostals, Anglicans, nondenominational charismatics, Vineyards, Assemblies of God, Lutherans, Presbyterians, the United Church, no-official-status churches, house churches, Bible studies, mission outposts, urban ecumenical communal houses, Nazarenes, and all points in between. And as I traveled, I began to realize just how vast and beautiful, complicated, and unable to be categorized the Church is at her heart.

I met people who were better Christians than I'll ever hope to be, even though they never darkened the door of a church on Sunday mornings. They simply loved the person in front of them well and built friendships everywhere they went, worshipping, blessing, interceding, and doing good together. And I've met people who have been at the same church for a literal lifetime. What a beautiful story.

You deserve belonging, beloved. You need community. You need siblings and friends, mothers and fathers whether by blood or by choice, saucy aunties and casual acquaintances to remember our names at the coffee shop, and you still need some way to give and some way to receive. Life will always be a communal experience. And even if you don't identify as a

Christian any longer, you still need people. You need your people. However it looks, I think the question to ask is less about finding a new church and dealing with the fallout from your old church or wherever you find yourself spinning out right now. Rather, ask yourself, Where am I finding belonging right now? And where can I create belonging for others, too?

It's always going to be a risk. Community is a risk; friendship and love are risks.

Against all odds and evidence, I still believe in intentional community. In fact, our family is slowly and probably overcautiously attending a new church, and once again, I'm hopeful and I'm scared. I have learned my lesson about placing a period where God has put a comma, but I keep trying. For me, it has helped to surrender many of my expectations for the ideals, make peace with the realities, and simply carve out a space between them both for *possibility*.

YOU MIGHT BE SURPRISED
WHERE YOU BELONG

Belonging won't require you to become less of yourself. True belonging celebrates the fullness of who you are, all of it. Dr. Chanequa Walker-Barnes called out the tendency to make ourselves fit into communities where we were perhaps never meant to fit. At Evolving Faith one year, she asked, "What would it look like if I stopped trying to fit? What would it look like if I embraced being fitless?"[6]

Sometimes the very things that mean you don't belong in church will be the pathway for belonging in other places and with other people. You aren't limited to churches when it comes to finding your belonging. You'll learn to find, or create, your own little island of misfit toys,* and it will be beautiful. Not all of us return to traditional church as we perhaps understood it, and our reasons are as unique as we are.

But by the same token, I do know that there are good churches where you can find belonging even when you don't entirely fit in. I know there are churches that will welcome you for the very gifts or questions or decisions that got you kicked out of another church. Even if it's just for a short season in your life, there are churches who will love you and your people. You'll eat together and baptize each other and ask good questions. Professor and author David Gushee offers this advice:

> My counsel to my fellow post-evangelicals is simply this: keep looking until you find the group of Christ's people that is a good fit for you. You will have your own set of nonnegotiables that you might be looking for; here is mine. Seek out a flesh-and-blood local community of covenanted believers who are seriously committed to following Jesus and seeking his kingdom together, who reflect and seek Christian unity, holiness, catholicity (for all, including LGBTQ+ people), and apostolicity. Seek out a community where you can experience the love of God and people. Christ alive and active on the earth, the loving presence of God's Spirit, people doing kingdom work, support for your journey, and serious nourishment through Scripture, worship, and sacrament. Look for a place where you can make a covenant commitment to real people for the long term. Then do that.[7]

---

* Rankin/Bass Christmas movies forever and amen. The weirder the better, in my opinion.

I would add only that it's possible to have this same experience without being in person, as we learned during the pandemic, and as many folks who live much of their connected lives online for many reasons, including disability, have often reminded us. You can also find a very real community through a computer, and that's just as holy, especially when you live in a place without a lot of church options.

You might find your belonging in an alternative community, like a book club or a Pilates studio, a knitting circle or an online affinity group, a hiking club or a volunteering opportunity. You'll find and build, contribute to and fund, show up for and scrap with all the places you find belonging. As Dr. Chanequa Walker-Barnes concluded:

> Our journeys may require us to remove ourselves from little "c" church for a while, but we are still part of the church universal. We remain tethered to it, even if it's only through our calls for a new reformation. So occasionally, if you are inside the church walls, you may hear us on the outside, slowly chiseling away, trying to create a new opening into which we and all God's people can bring our entire selves.

Therapy and relationship coaching can help you learn how to handle the specifics of your situation, but it almost always begins with establishing boundaries on your new map of life. Needing to take some space or establish boundaries isn't about sorting people into good and bad piles in your mind. That sort of reductionist othering wasn't helpful to you before, and it won't serve you now either. You can let people be complicated, let your feelings toward them hold nuance, and you can establish boundaries without hatefulness, cruelty, or reduction of folks to enemies. Boundaries are a way to love each other—and ourselves—well. As boundaries expert Nedra Glover Tawwab writes, "Some people aren't good for you, and they aren't bad people."[8]

And then there are friends who will evolve with you, fortunately. Professor and author Brené Brown calls these "stretch mark friends," which is a metaphor I understand deeply after four babies. "Our connection has been stretched and pulled so much that it's become part of who we are, a second skin, and there are a few scars to prove it,"[9] she says. For what it's worth, most of us have only one or two friends who reach this level of friendship. Not every relationship can be a stretch mark friend, so if you have one, bless that, too. I hope I don't miss the opportunity to be that sort of friend to others, too.

Wherever you're finding belonging right now, it matters because you matter. Don't worry so much about whether or not it's okay or whether or not it "counts" in some weird cosmic score chart you've assigned to God.

Here's the thing I want to say most of all: it's okay. You can release the deep breath you're holding. And you don't need to be afraid you're getting it wrong. You might not belong where you once did, but that doesn't mean you don't belong anywhere. You're part of a vast company out here in the wilderness, a whole expanse of people who haven't fit and don't fit. There are many ways to find and cultivate belonging, friend. You'll find your spot and you'll be someone else's harbor.

You can sit by me,
S.

Chapter 12

LOOK FOR GOOD TEACHERS

Dear Curious,

There is a story in the book of Matthew where Jesus tells us to beware of false prophets, who come to us in sheep's clothing but inwardly are ravenous wolves. "You will know them by their fruits," he says. "Are grapes gathered from thorns, or figs from thistles? In the same way, every good tree bears good fruit, but the bad tree bears bad fruit. A good tree cannot bear bad fruit, nor can a bad tree bear good fruit." He concludes with the line that has become a North Star for me, "You will know them by their fruits."*

I suspect that at least part of the reason you've landed here in the wilderness, filled with despair and doubt and stories, is that you've encountered a few wolves in sheep's clothing and you've been consuming bad fruit for too long. Discernment of good fruit is something you're going to have to learn out here, especially if you've spent a lifetime denying your own intuition and inner knowing in the service of someone else's idea of the greater good. If you don't know which fruits are safe to eat and which ones will poison you, you're in danger. It's just that too many of us have spent too long being told the rotten fruit we're eating is actually good. Our little discerners are a bit messed up, aren't they? For too long, we've been expected to toe the

* Matthew 7:15–20 NRSV.

party line of our denomination or our particular church without question.

Sometimes it's religious leaders who gaslight us into believing that bad fruit is actually good fruit. I see this with a lot of theology designed to keep women from leading, preaching, or functioning as full equals in the world, the church, and their homes. It bears bad fruit, patriarchy does, and we see that in the marginalized lives of women all around the world. Calling something good doesn't make it good. Calling patriarchy God's plan or dressing it up with sacred language doesn't make it so.

I'd say the same thing about unaffirming theology. We are often told that being unaffirming of LGBTQ+ folks is good theology, but time after time we see the true results of that policy, and it's bad fruit, it just is. It's bad fruit that excludes vulnerable people, makes teenagers want to die, estranges families, and results in shame, self-loathing, and cruelty at best, murder and abuse and oppression at worst. As my dear friend Jen Hatmaker wryly shared at one Evolving Faith conference, "Those were the tough breaks of subscribing to a tough gospel under a pretty tough God. It was the ultimate case of gaslighting; 'Your heart is not broken because we broke it with terrible theology. It is broken because of your errors. Therefore, we declare all this bad fruit good.'"[1]

LOOK AT THE FRUIT

Having spent a fair bit of time being labeled a heretic and a wolf in sheep's clothing myself, I know that it's painful, and I am not so ungenerous as to believe that everyone who disagrees with me or you is a wolf in sheep's clothing by any stretch.

Rather, I think we need listen to Jesus* and "look at the fruit."
Those words come at the conclusion of one of his most famous
sermons, the Sermon on the Mount. Originally from the Greek
word *dokimazō*, which means "to weigh," this expression was
used in the context of figuring out which metals were real and
which were fake. Over time it became a word that we use to
figure out what's true and what's false.[2] The call for discernment often shows up in the New Testament because people
were figuring out in real time what was true and what was false
about Jesus, about the Church, about Scripture, and about
how to live in this world. Paul wrote to the Philippians to "determine what is best, so that in the day of Christ you may be
pure and blameless," yes, but he preceded this advice with the
prayer that their "love may overflow more and more with
knowledge and full insight" in that work.† We can't do good
discernment work without overflowing love alongside that
knowledge and insight.

So part of what we're learning here in the wilderness is how
to discern again. We need to learn who to trust, who to question, and how to live. It's not even that we lack knowledge—
although that may be true, especially if we came of age in a
spiritual or political or communal echo chamber. But it's perhaps also that we lack the love as we do this discerning work.

In the New Testament,‡ Paul tells us what the fruits of the
Spirit are, and it's not too complicated really: love, joy, peace,
patience, kindness, generosity, faithfulness, gentleness, and
self-control. Sometimes we can overthink things; I'm tired of

---

* Pro tip: this is usually a good idea.
† Philippians 1:10, 1:9 NRSV.
‡ Galatians 5:22–23 NRSV.

the mental and spiritual gymnastics that require us to contort ourselves into believing anything other than the nine qualities Paul lists is good fruit.

Look for the places and people where you're experiencing love. Watch out for joy and lean into peacemaking. When you find people who are patient and kind, pay attention. When someone's teaching is increasing the goodness not only in you but in the world, notice it. If there isn't gentleness and self-control, especially in our interactions with one another, maybe most especially among those with whom we disagree, I think it matters. I'm not interested in being discipled in outrage. We don't need more selfish and impatient role models. This world isn't crying out for more division and brokenness. Nope, we're good, thanks.

Look for what is bringing life and flourishing into the world. In short, look at the fruit. If the fruit of a movement or a community or a leader is more hatred, more division, less compassion, especially for those who aren't at the center of the conversation in politics and history and government, church and social services and economics, then we need to stop consuming or passing around that bad fruit.

REORIENTING OURSELVES

It has served me so well to find good teachers here in the wilderness, and I believe it will serve you, too. However, what I mean by "good teachers" might need some expansion. For too long we've established highly educated, white, western, straight, powerful, married, able-bodied, male voices as the primary and preferred teachers in the room. They have been the center of our texts, education, and understanding for a long time.

I genuinely don't think we'll be able to move forward in honesty and wholeness and flourishing without reorienting the center of God's geography from the dominant, majority, powerful ones toward the ones sidelined, marginalized, and ignored. We need to reorient ourselves to where we really reside in the story. I speak here particularly to those who share a form of identity with me.* When you are part of the majority, the ones historically at the center of everything from theological work to government to business to art, you can have a rather insular interpretive community.

So, if we're looking for good fruit, we also need to look at who benefits. That's why we need to ask ourselves if the Good News is actually good news *for everyone.* If it isn't good news for someone who is not at the historical center of power and privilege, then it isn't good news, is it? And if we're enjoying a lot of privilege, it's almost always on the back of someone else, whether we acknowledge that or not, whether it was our decision or not.

We have our work cut out for us because if we have been privileged and centered and empowered, then we've also been told that our way of reading Scripture or doing church or moving through the world is the right one, the scriptural one, the biblical one. And that isn't always true. We still belong, don't mistake me, we're still beloved and capable and invited. It's just perhaps also time to remember that privilege and power are rarely the best tools for discerning the truth. Theologian and author Kelley Nikondeha writes,

---

* Those of us who are white or are western or are well educated; those of us who have some measure of privilege because of our age or our body or our marital status or our income level even.

Engaging our social imagination is not something we do once and for all. Evaluating our privilege is a constant activity, much like the person in recovery who daily remembers that they must work in steps toward health and wholeness. We take stock, we strategize, and we partner with our neighbours for a more just world."[3]

I've encountered this reality in many ways over the past few years, but one in particular comes to my mind. When I was a kid coming up through the school system in Canada, we covered residential schools once or twice. Vaguely studied them, did a little paragraph about them with the same unconcern we used for the British North America Act or the arrival of Samuel de Champlain. It was a "dark chapter" in our history, we were told, a chapter that has been long closed, hardly worth more than a paragraph in our written-by-white-settlers history books. One hundred and thirty residential schools operated in many communities across Canada. As a matter of government policy over seven generations, the children of Indigenous families were systemically removed—kidnapped, really—from their families and taken to these residential schools far from their culture and community for the purpose of assimilation.

To us, this was a long time ago, it had nothing to do with us: we didn't notice the First Nations and Métis kids in our little classrooms had become very quiet and withdrawn while we copied notes and underreported statistics from the overhead projectors.

No one told us there were still residential schools open and operating at that blessed moment. No one named the truth that they weren't residential "schools," not really; they were state-sanctioned genocide concentration camps for children, explicitly intended to "kill the Indian in the child" and so erase Indigenous people and culture. We didn't know that more than 150,000 First Nations, Métis, and Inuit kids between the ages of four and sixteen were sent to these schools while they were in operation. And that similar schools existed across the United States, Australia, and other colonized countries.

Seven generations of Indigenous children were removed from their homes, their parents, their communities, and their families to be placed in these government-sponsored religious schools as an act of colonization. Children were stolen from their mothers, forbidden to speak their language, cut off from their culture and way of life, separated from their families, malnourished, worked relentlessly. More than 90 percent of them were abused physically, sexually, spiritually, and emotionally. Conservative estimates place the mortality rate at 50 to 60 percent for these kids. What's sobering is that the last residential school in Canada closed in 1996—basically yesterday.

It wasn't until I was in my late thirties that I learned of the Sixties Scoop, another government-sponsored policy toward Indigenous children. Once the residential schools fell out of favor, the government and churches began to quietly close them, instead opting to remove Indigenous children from their homes and families to be fostered and adopted by non-Indigenous families. Not only were these children—again—taken from their parents and grandparents but they were stolen from their way of life, their culture, their language, their heritage, often at the mercy of the foster care system. Even their names were often lost.

A friend of mine who was herself taken by the Scoop testifies about sisters and brothers she's never met, a mother who fell apart in their absence (who wouldn't?), grandparents who died without ever knowing where she was or if she had even survived, and the nights of loneliness and devastating grief she endured as a *four-year-old*, taken from the only life she knew and dropped into a whole new world.

My friend is only a few years older than I am. We are of the same generation.

In 2020, just a few hours away from where my family lived at the time, a mass grave was discovered at a former residential school. The technology available to us now confirmed what the elders and survivors had tried to tell Canada for years: in that grave were the bodies of 215 children. Most of the children were unidentified. Generations of Indigenous elders, activists, and witnesses knew that this site and others like it all across Canada exist. The truth was sitting in volume 4 of the Truth and Reconciliation Commission's report[4] right then and it still is. Some of the children in that mass grave were as young as three years old. There was never justice for these kids and their families.

So, there is fruit that was once called good. It is the fruit of colonization and cruelty. Maybe it was purposely erased, buried, hidden, silenced, but it is the rotten fruit. And when it comes to looking for good teachers, we have to be able to tell the truth about the fruit.

AN INVITATION TO SOMETHING TRUE

When we look for good teachers, we're really being invited to grapple with truth. We're being invited into reality, a reality that has been going on alongside our building programs and Sunday schools and fundraising and charity suppers. We're being invited into our origin story, into the complex and complicated truth of our histories and their ongoing rotten legacy.

Consider whose theology and version of the story has shaped you up until now. Look at your bookshelves, your podcasts, your music, your teachers, your friendships, your understanding of history. Are they pretty much the same? They usually are. And that's not to discount the goodness you may have found there—although you have likely also encountered a lot of garbage. It's simply to say that you are invited into something new now. You're invited to be intentional about your teachers now. Look for the teachers you've been missing. Look for the ones telling the truth to power. Look for the stories you haven't heard yet. You're invited to participate in making things right as you learn. Consider whose theology is shaping you and adjust accordingly.

My friend Kaitlin Curtice, a citizen of the Potawatomi Nation, writes,

> Decolonization is not just for the oppressed. It is a gift for everyone. Just as growing pains hurt before the actual growth takes place, so it hurts to decolonize. For some, it hurts like hell, and then one day, we all appear on the other side of it, healed, our stories told in all their truth. Just like that, we all gather to bathe in the healing waters, and just like that, everyone is made clean.[5]

If you've been formed by only one particular voice or experience or social location, then you're missing so much of what makes God beautiful and true, good and loving. I love and know and follow Jesus better when I'm listening to Black womanists and when I hear how a gay man from a Southern Baptist church learned to believe he was loved by God and when I attend a community powwow. When I hear how a Haitian woman experiences God's faithfulness, and when I hear from first-generation believers, nursing mothers, and grieving husbands. When I hear from survivors of residential schools, cancer patients in chemotherapy treatment, carpenters, and gardeners. When I hear from people who are outside the gates, outside the usual power and leadership and privilege narratives.

Dr. Soon-Chan Rah writes,

> Fifty years ago, if you were asked to describe a typical Christian in the world, you could confidently assert that person to be an upper middle-class, white male, living in an affluent and comfortable Midwest suburb. If you were to ask the same question today, that answer would more likely be a young Nigerian mother on the outskirts of Lagos, a university student in Seoul, South Korea, or a teenage boy in Mexico City. European and North American Christianity continue to decline, while African, Asian, and Latin-American Christianity continue to increase dramatically . . . Global Christianity is clearly non-white.[6]

Some of the greatest theologians we'll meet are ordinary people who aren't writing books, preaching on stages, or teaching at schools. They're our grandmothers in prayer circles, our next-door neighbors, our fellow wanderers in the wilderness, the church rejects, the Bible nerds, the artists, our children, our friends, midwives breathing with laboring women; and each of them has a story to tell about why they know what they know

now about God. When we listen to these voices, we're free to be as the Berean Jews in Acts 17, who "received the message with great eagerness and examined the Scriptures every day to see if what Paul said was true."*

On the other side of finding good teachers, there is that constant invitation from God to participate. To participate in making things right, to participate in healing and repentance, to participate in goodness. We'll talk more about this in the coming chapters.

Remember, we're looking for good fruit. We're looking for people to flourish. We're looking for teachers and teachings that bring honor and goodness and joy. We're looking for truth-tellers, elders, and the rest of the story. Listen, listen, to the many voices singing God's goodness and welcome that we've silenced and ignored for too long. There is a whole choir out here.

Taste and see,
S.

* Acts 17:11 NIV.

Chapter 13

BECOME A NEW EXPLORER
ON AN ANCIENT PATH

Dear Pathfinder,

A few years ago, our family of six packed up our house, our family, and our two cats,* and moved to a new province. We had been in British Columbia for more than fifteen years by then, but for a dozen reasons, it was time for a change. So we upped-sticks, as we say, and moved to Calgary, Alberta, which is where I grew up.

Moving is terrible, don't let anyone tell you differently. The only bright spot is that it does have an end date: at some point, you are done with the moving. It doesn't go on forever. One day, all the boxes will be unpacked and you will be settled, but it just takes a long, long, long time to get there. And then a bit longer to figure out things like finding a doctor and the post office and a friend.

Among the eleventy-billion other details that went into moving provinces, we spent weeks sorting through the stuff of our lives. We sold furniture, housewares, and tools on Facebook Marketplace, took a few loads to the dump, shredded and recycled reams of paper. We reduced and recycled, gave away, and donated like it was our job as we packed for this major transition. Marie Kondo would have been so proud of us. We

---

* Amy and Rory, and yes, they were named for two well-loved companions on the TV show *Doctor Who*.

purged and cleaned and tossed our worldly possessions with abandon.

And yet? It turned out I loved my stuff. Books, teacups, papers, the scrapbook of cutout pictures from bridal magazines that functioned as an analog version of Pinterest for my era of wedding planning—it surprised me how hard it was to throw any of this away.

Loving our stuff has gone a bit off popularity these days. We're modern minimalists with clean lines and empty shelves. We're trying experiments like having only one hundred things in our homes. We're enchanted with tiny houses that have small footprints. I find these minimalist movements inspiring. I see the benefits and the truth of the philosophy behind the purging. A major move is certainly one way to sober you up about the amount of stuff you have. And yes, most of us have too much stuff, even if you aren't a collecting magpie like one of our daughters, whose room became an excavation site of glitter, seashells, and Barbie shoes. By the time we had loaded the moving van, I had developed a wonderful rant about consumerism and overspending, clutter and entitled consumption, so let me know if you want to hear that sometime.

Over the years, I've certainly embraced a simpler way of life. I am the type of person who is more settled in a tidy home with clear kitchen counters; clutter drives me bonkers. I get so overwhelmed at big-box stores my husband has taken to leaving me behind when it's time to get something at IKEA because of my deer-in-the-headlights expression and sweaty palms. (It is a joy being married to me.)

Like many of us, I also try to be intentional and thoughtful about justice issues, even in everyday purchases, like our clothing and food and furniture. I believe in living within our means, certainty, and be guaranteed desired outcomes.* It was an invitation to control, never surrender. Spoiler alert: this practice of prayer was decidedly not great—theologically, spiritually, physically, emotionally, mentally, or, you know, for any person with a real life in the real world.

It took losing prayer altogether for me to have the space to imagine prayer anew, to learn to leave room for silence in prayer. Even the phrase "thoughts and prayers" being posted on social media after another mass shooting or another preventable tragedy is enough to fill me with rage, because who wants thoughts and prayers instead of action and engagement?

It was only through time and space, conversation and good teachers, even a bit of glorious desperation that I began to expand my definition of prayer. I began taking ancient paths of prayer, ones I had never encountered before, like walking labyrinths and lighting candles and holding vigil. I began to pick up prayers by others, written for my grief and sorrow and longing. I learned about liturgy at the same time that good anger and long silence became part of my spiritual practice. I began the work of listening and discovered that it, too, could be prayer. In so doing I discovered there was room for reality, for hospital rooms and unanswered prayers and unspoken needs and broken hearts now. I learned about prayer from rivers running through rocky valleys and the feeling in my throat when I watched the sun set over the mountains to the west. I learned about prayer from my son, who once told me that he just sits with Jesus sometimes. If you've ever sat in companionable silence with a friend,† you know the sort of prayer I often pray these days.

---

* If you want to read more about this, you can in *Out of Sorts: Making Peace with an Evolving Faith* as well as *Miracles and Other Reasonable Things*.
† I tell this story in my book *Miracles and Other Reasonable Things*.

purchasing with intention and frequent visits to secondhand shops when possible, and I believe in being unreasonably generous.

But I still love my stuff.

I love the teacups my Granny Styles gave to me, along with her kitchen knickknacks, decorative plates, the battered copies of her favorite Zane Grey and Jalna novels. Her slender, violently orange ceramic cat, which presided over her kitchen sink from the windowsill, now rests in my kitchen. I love collecting the vintage editions of L. M. Montgomery books I stumble across in secondhand stores. (Boxes of fragile hundred-year-old hardcovers traveled in my minivan with me over the mountains, no risky moving van for them.) The first stories I ever wrote are still tucked away, along with my embarrassing high school and college journals, which my sister is, Cassandra Austen–like, under a covenant to burn if I meet an untimely demise. My mother's old dishes, the first dress I bought for our first baby, the love letters my husband wrote to me when we started dating in the late nineties. I adore our beat-up kitchen table with the shabby chairs, and almost every week, I use the white teapot with a little blue flower on the side that I bought in Germany so long ago.

It's not about the things themselves, not really. It's about the stories of the stuff and the way I want to embody those stories in our home.

I loved my complicated grandmother, and having her things around me reminds me of the line of fierce, deep-thinking, take-no-shit women that I come from. The L. M. Montgomery books profoundly shaped my girlhood and my way of seeing the world with eyes of hope, wonder, goodness—each one I find on a crowded charity shop shelf feels like a rescue. That gigantic poplar kitchen table fits the whole family, and I love it so much, not just because of the function of the thing itself but because of what it represents to me: family, gathering at the table, space for a few more friends, laughter. The water rings and scorch marks are testimonies of togetherness, and all the people I love most near me while they eat the good food we've prepared together. That white teapot is an icon of one of the most difficult seasons of our life, because the trip to Germany itself reset our entire trajectory as a result of the sorrows of miscarriage and the strange beginnings of my own deconstruction. It's functional, yes, but it's also a tangible representation of my own before-and-after spiritual life, the deep grief our marriage has weathered together, and the possibility of another morning.

The things I have kept over the years honor memories and bring me joy, and so I kept them. Even KonMari approves of this method.[1]

I believe there is room in our homes—and in our lives—for more than just the useful or functional: there is room for the lovely, the memory-filled, the beautiful, the sacred, the just-because-I-love-it-still stuff. So even though I consider myself someone who practices intentional living, I still surround myself with the familiar things. I've discovered that I'm not the type of person who can live as a minimalist, not really.

KEEP, TOSS, REPURPOSE

We can find metaphors in so many corners of our lives. I have had similar "Marie Kondo" experiences as part of my evolving faith. As I've rummaged through what I believe over the years, and I've slowly figured out what needs to go and what needs to stay, I have certainly thrown out beliefs and practices and opinions that were no longer serving me or the world.

And yet I have found myself reclaiming so much of what I thought I had outgrown, too. It turned out that many things I had once scorned were actually precious to me. Sometimes I've been surprised by what I've held on to, reenchanted by their beauty once I was able to perceive these things from a new vantage point.

An evolving faith doesn't mean we burn down everything that was once precious to us. There is something between everything and nothing. We aren't required to toss everything we were taught or given as "worthless" or "useless" or even "toxic" as we grow and change, becoming more fully ourselves. There is room to honor and hold space for the precious and the meaningful even as we evolve in our beliefs, our homes, and our lives. It's okay to bring some things with you.

For me, part of the work of the wilderness has been to learn to listen well to those who have walked these paths ahead of me. In spite of all the hand-wringing over deconstruction these days, it's not a new phenomenon, nor are we without guides, companions, and even friends on this path. Sometimes while we wander, we find old stories, old treasures, old paths, old friends, and we realize, *Oh, this is precious, too. I think I want to bring this with me.*

Pastor and theologian A. J. Swoboda writes, "To move forward, we must remember. We don't jettison the past. We honour it, receive it, listen to it. God's people best move forward into the future by intentionally retrieving the past."[2]

One of the reasons I have a few items from my granny is that I asked for them. I went to visit her near the end of her life, right about the time that she was breaking up housekeeping in order to move into a seniors' home. She was clearly wistful about her things: she hadn't had any daughters, she said, and what did her three grown boys want with old china and photo albums, vintage handkerchiefs and novels from the 1940s? At the end of her life, she wanted someone to want her things, to see them as being as precious as she did. She wanted to tell the stories behind them and place them into someone's hands for safekeeping. *Here, this is the one I bought with my first paycheck in the city after I left the farm. This is the photo of my nephew Billy, the last one I have because he died in a car accident just a few weeks later, he was such a beautiful boy. Here is the novel I bought from the library bookmobile van sale in the late seventies. Here, this is the decorative plate that I kept in my china cabinet, I don't think I ever used it, but I should have.* Over and over, she entrusted her stories to my open hands.

It was easy to love her things because I loved her. I asked for a few keepsakes and told her I'd keep them always. I tucked a small box of items into the front seat of my car, brought them home and unpacked them, blended them into our family's still unfolding stories.

I wonder sometimes about what we might reclaim out here. I wonder if there are things you thought you'd leave behind that might become precious to you. I wonder if there is a way for you to love things simply because people you love have loved them.

Don't be too quick to toss everything. You might be surprised what becomes precious to you over time.

REIMAGINING PRAYER

I have found a lot of freedom in reimagining certain aspects of my faith in order to hang on to them. There is a lot more room to play than we were told; there is room for imagination and wonder and embrace. There is room for our traditions or practices, beliefs or spiritual disciplines to evolve with us.

Prayer is one of my own great passions and practices, which can surprise people. Sometimes it reminds me of the days back when Brian and I were in a Texas megachurch and it would come up in conversation that I was a feminist. People would sort of cock their heads and this confused expression would appear on their faces because, well, they had a picture in their minds of what a scary feminist would look like in real life—thanks to stereotypes and fear-mongering media or Christian leaders. And I? Well, I didn't seem to fit the bill.*

Sometimes I see that same bewildered expression on people's faces when I talk about prayer. There is a particular kind of person they imagine as a woman of prayer, and me? Well, *do wishy-washy progressives and those libs even, like, pray?* their faces telegraph. But I love to pray, only prayer now just looks a bit different than the way I was raised to do it.

I don't know if I'll pray the way that I was taught in my Word of Faith churches ever again. Praying for specific outcomes, claiming things of God, Bible verses as reminders, watching confession, demanding God's intervention in the ways that I see fit—all of it is gone, and good riddance. I used to think of prayer as a cosmic vending machine: pray the right way, with the right words, without doubt and with absolute

---

* If you are a scary feminist who fits the bill, my congratulations and admiration. I aspire.

If you've given up on prayer, I encourage you to crack open a bit of possibility for reimagination. Sometimes your wordless longings are the purest prayer. Sometimes your fist shaking at heaven, your demand for God to wake up and do something, is a prayer—you're praying like a Psalmist now. Sometimes your joy, your laughter, your delight are better than any formal prayer of thanksgiving. Sometimes your quiet resignation and lack of faith in anything to change is its own conversation with the God who hears, too.

In these days of powers and principalities, these days of apocalypse even, prayer can also become the very entryway to ordering the universe again. Rabbi Abraham Joshua Heschel says,

> Prayer is meaningless unless it is subversive, unless it seeks to overthrow and ruin pyramids of callousness, hatred, opportunism, falsehoods. The liturgical movement must become a revolutionary movement, seeking to overthrow the forces that continue to destroy the promise, the hope, the vision.[3]

Good teachers have shown me that prayer isn't inactivity or passivity, an opposite to action and engagement; it is one more practice to keep us rooted to God and one another as we go on loving in the face of fear, contending for hope in the midst of despair, fighting for justice in our world. Prayer keeps us engaged with God, with the work, and with each other. It's not being nostalgic or invoking magic spells or sticking our heads in the sand; it is our engagement, our invitation, our practice of paying attention.

The most beautiful part of prayer to me now is the knowledge that it isn't a monologue. Prayer is a conversation of love, moving you through your life as it is now, even now.

Here's another tradition I've reclaimed: prayer cloths. Oh, this one makes me cackle. Back in the day, saints used to hold on to a little scrap of fabric while they prayed. Sometimes they anointed their snippet with oil. And then they would give it to the person for whom they had been praying. It was meant to be a tangible representation of their prayers, a way to tuck people's petitions into your pocket and keep it with you when you went to the hospital, for instance. But the practice became a bit of a running joke by the eighties, thanks to televangelists who sold prayer cloths to their viewers. For just nine dollars, you, too, could have a scrap of white fabric that they "promised" had been prayed over by the fancy man of God on the TV. I found it abhorrent. Exploitive, silly, manipulative, fake.

Well, fast-forward thirty years . . . A dear friend was in the midst of great heartbreak and upheaval as her twenty-six-year marriage was ending abruptly and traumatically. Everything in me longed to be with her. I wanted to sit on the end of the couch and listen to every word she had to say. I wanted to lie in the bed and keep watch while she cried herself to sleep, I wanted to cook good meals in her kitchen. But because of the pandemic, I couldn't be with her and the thought of her, alone, at her house, was turning me inside out. I prayed for her, I called her, but somehow it wasn't enough.

One day, I found one of my granny's old handkerchiefs in my jewelry box and I had a ridiculous thought: what if I held it while I prayed for my friend? I found a tiny bottle of olive oil from Palestine someone had sent as a gift; I guessed that would do. Every time I prayed for my friend, I touched a bit of oil on the cloth and I cried. When she and I talked on the phone, I held that same cloth. After a few weeks, I carefully folded up the handkerchief and mailed it to her along with a note that read, "You are who we knew you to be. I imagine you held in the love and embrace of God who broods over you like a mother." I explained what I had done with this little scrap of fabric, how it was an embodiment of my prayers for her and my love for her. To this day, it sits on her desk, within arm's reach.

I never imagined myself reembracing and reimagining something as "silly" as prayer cloths; I don't think the one I gave to my friend was magic or even particularly miraculous. But it was a tangible way to tell her I loved her and that I was with her, and even that feels like Jesus to me. I don't know what I believe about what that was, not exactly, but I know that I needed an outlet for love and she needed to receive a tangible expression of love and this did it for us.

I can't tell you what is precious and what should be discarded. (Well, I mean I can, but I probably shouldn't. Look at me, I'm growing!) I'll just say this: stay open. Stay open to ancient paths and old wisdom and good saints. Stay open to Bible verses you loved when you were a kid and the songs that you still sing at night when you think no one can hear you. You don't have to make fun of everything you used to love, and you certainly don't need to despise it. Handle your old ways with gentleness. You might find something to love here eventually.

Even if you do end up leaving behind all of what you once practiced, you can spare a bit of compassion for the version of you who loved those things and needed them. Perhaps you can offer some kindness to the ones who still love them, too.

Even among the ancient paths, there is more room to wander than you were told. There are so many beautiful, complicated, twisty, weird, old ways to love God and love people. It might look different than it did, it might be a bit outside the lines, but it's an old path and you belong on it, too.

A grandmother at heart,
S.

Chapter 14

REMEMBER TO BE FOR, NOT JUST AGAINST

Dear Scrappy One,

One of the values we have at Evolving Faith is to practice being "for" things, not just against things. We often start with the latter, and that is a good start. Dismantling powers and principles, injustices and damage is good work to do. But it doesn't end there.

I remember author Elizabeth Gilbert once sharing that the feeling of "not this" is a good beginning.[1] Almost all of us have a moment of realizing that we're in what she calls "the wrong place—or at least, in a very bad place." It might be your marriage, your church, your beliefs, your habits, your addictions, your choices, your government, whatever. Then there is the moment of realization: *not this*. Not anymore anyway. It's scary and awful, but it's also very brave to say it out loud and to let your life reflect it. Especially when we don't know what's next or what could be coming or even what we hope for yet, but we simply know it's *not this*.

We often find our way to the wilderness because of the dawning realization of our "not this," and it becomes our Against.

Against the rise of conspiracy theories and Christian nationalism. Against the anointing of wickedness. Against the gaslighting of calling something good fruit when it clearly is rotten. Against police brutality. Against purity culture. Against ableism. Against fat phobia. Against burnout glorification. Against the denial of climate change. We could do this all day, eh?

Those are big Againsts, but they often begin smaller than that, don't they? We often start with our own quiet Against, the one in our lives. It may not even be a big theological thing, certainly not a geopolitical thing. It begins with our own knowing, our own lives, our own choices. We may not be able to say *I'm against patriarchy* at first, but we know that we're against being paid less at work because of our sex. We may not be able to articulate that we're against purity culture, but we begin by knowing we're against calling people "damaged goods" or debating yoga pants on social media.*

Sometimes the Against rises up in us to such a volume that we turn away even before we know what we're turning toward. It is the part of our soul that cries out against anything that reduces or diminishes the image-of-God-ness in each other. In my conversations with folks, I've heard so many stories of their own Against awakenings, from church splits to the lack of a baby shower for a pregnant teenager in the youth group, from a school shooting to an election, from a Bible study that teaches women to be more submissive to their abusers to refusing to bake a cake for a gay couple. It can be anything in your life. I don't know the specifics, but I know right now you're thinking of what caused your own Against to awaken, ringing the dinner bell of *Enough!* in your heart.

You don't know what you're for, not yet, you just know that it isn't this, it couldn't possibly be *this*.

Surely God is better than this, we think. Right?

---

* Why, oh, why do all the hot takes on women wearing yoga pants come from a guy with "husband/father/pastor/IPA drinker" in their bio?

It's holy, good work to identify your Against, so I bless it. Your Against awakening has served you so far and it matters. Whatever it was that hurt you or those you loved matters. Whatever it was that caused you to pay attention to your own desires and hopes matters. Whatever it was that made you turn away from broken systems and damaging theology matters.

I just want you to remember that it's good to name and seek to embody what you're *for* as well.

JOURNEY TOWARD

If you spend any amount of time with the Hebrew Bible, you quickly realize: it's filled with people on the move. From Abram's initial departure from the land of his fathers to Jacob's journey after his betrayal of his brother, Esau. From Joseph's journey to Egypt after being sold into slavery by his brothers to those same brothers' journey to Egypt to ask for food from the very brother they betrayed. There is the journey of Moses out of Egypt after he commits murder, Aaron's journey into the wilderness to find that same brother. Moses leads his people out of Egypt to wander in the wilderness for forty years, a journey that seems unending. Hannah going to the temple with Samuel, Esther pacing a palace for such a time as this, Deborah journeying to war and the glory of battle victory. Journeys overflow throughout Scripture when you start to see the pattern—and so this journey of yours has good company.

Journeys abound in our myths and in our stories for a reason. Leo Tolstoy reportedly once said that there are only two stories we tell: someone goes on a journey or a stranger comes to town.[2] Even the mythic "hero's journey" trope as explored by Joseph Campbell leans into this pattern—the three main stages of a hero's journey are the departure (our hero leaves their place of origin), then the initiation (the trials and challenges, friends and enemies, of the new place turn our protagonist into a hero), and then the triumphant return.[3] We see it in literature and movies from *The Lion King* to *Doctor Who* to *Eat Pray Love*. Of course, there are more than a dozen other steps along the way, from refusing the quest to finding a mentor to resurrection, too.

The wilderness is where we begin to set down the beautiful and terrible burdens we carry—we grow tired of lugging them to the new spaces of our souls, and the thing we couldn't imagine ever releasing ends up at the side of the road, abandoned with hardly a backward glance. Freedom becomes more important than clinging to the things that don't belong in this wild and starlit place. But every single one of those items you used to cherish—your cynicism, your hypocrisy, your lies, your numbing techniques, your apologetics and doctrinal statements, your worldview, your opinions, your carefully constructed personas, your sins, your righteousness, your secrets, your new freedoms and current masters, the new opinions you traded for the old ones with the same fundamentalist fervor, the things inflicted upon you, the well-meaning lies—all of them become filthy rags, and in the end, you are nearly flinging them off.

It seems to me that a lot of God's people spent time in one wilderness or another, literal or metaphorical, and they rarely assumed the comfort of certainty so I've come to view this notion of a journey a bit differently. And that is because of one additional word: *toward.*

Don't forget to journey *toward.*

Because in all of the years wandering in the wilderness of my faith, it took a very long time for me to be quiet enough to hear the Spirit whispering, "So. This is nice. Now where are we going?"

You may well laugh. I know I do—kindly, gently—now. I had no idea. I knew what I was leaving. I knew that which lay behind me—or thought I did. But the reorienting of my wandering as not "fleeing from" but "journeying toward" was a reset I desperately needed.

What are we journeying toward out here in the wilderness?

I wanted then—and now—to journey toward my best hopes, not my worst fears. I want to journey toward redemption. Toward love, joy, peace, patience, kindness, goodness, faithfulness, gentleness, even self-control. Toward compassion and empathy. Toward justice and renewal. Toward equality and inclusion. Toward celebration and sorrow. Toward creation and possibility. Toward Jesus. Toward the margins where God is already quite at home. Truly toward one another.

I still wander now and then. I have grown to like it. I have grown to love the untamed places of my soul, and I like to walk in them alone, like a Brontë haunting the moors. But I've learned the fog will eventually give way to reveal what I'm moving toward.

I want that for all of us in the wilderness—to keep in mind that the journey we're on is still *toward*. Toward our true name. Toward our real home light. Toward deliverance. Toward freedom. Toward truth. Toward reconciliation. Toward peace. Toward one another. Toward our own self. Toward the great, abiding lovingkindness that even now faithfully holds us all right through the night.

IMAGINE SOMETHING BETTER

Imagining and contending for what you hope for in this world is one of the hardest and kindest paths I've discovered out here. In the midst of all this, don't forget to imagine something better. Don't forget to dream of what could be possible. And don't forget to live into those hopes with faithfulness. Move in that direction, especially when all you know is "not this."

If it helps, sometimes I've thought of this as the rhythm of turning away and then turning toward, almost like a beautiful dance. This turning away/toward has echoes of the metanoia we covered in our chat about repentance (see chapter 9). Just as metanoia shows us to turn away from sin and toward love, now we turn away from those things we're against and toward the hopeful future we imagine. In a purposeful movement, we turn away from the practices or beliefs or habits that consume us, threaten us, reduce us, and distract us. And then we turn toward what brings flourishing, goodness, and truth to us. Turn away, yes, and *turn toward*. Not this, and so *this*. It's a form of restoration. What we turn toward should reorient us to the world in a posture of love, joy, and service.

It can be a simple rhythm to begin with. Turning away from spaces in social media that have become toxic for you and turning toward inviting a lonely neighbor over for tea. Turning away from voices that bring shame and guilt to you or others and turning toward voices that preach freedom and wholeness and love. Or turning away from shrinking back and shutting up to keep the peace; turning toward owning your voice, your body, your experiences with boldness. Turning away from gossip and petty nitpicking; turning toward language of blessing. Turning away from a toxic relationship; turning toward devel-

oping healthy boundaries. Turning away from excuses and justifications; turning toward accountability.

Turning away is a good start, but it isn't going to sustain us
over the long haul. Naming what you are turning toward—
especially ordinary, good, lovely, nourishing things—is a rebel-
lion against the broken story itself.

An imperfect example? When I was growing up, we were
taught that if you gave money to the church or to the preacher,
then God was obligated and contract-bound to give money
back to you. Sowing and reaping; the harvest, pressed down,
shaken together, running back at thirty-, sixty-, hundredfold
returns. One of my earliest Againsts was this one: the manipulation and exploitation of preying on people's financial vulner-
abilities to encourage greed and consumerism. (Plus, it was just
a bad reading of the Bible.)

Because I was so Against the prosperity gospel, for a long
while I avoided any and all talk about money. I was Against the
abuses of it, against tithing as a formula and a guide for greed,
against the failure of the Church to care for the poor. But it
reached a point where I realized I didn't have a way to articulate
what I was For when it came to giving and generosity. Jesus
spoke often about generosity, about money, and even about
what theologians call "God's preferential option for the poor."[4]
I think this is part of the reason why Jesus tells us so clearly that
we can't serve both God and the love of money.* He is clear—no
one can serve two masters—you'll choose one or the other. It's
not that money is evil: it's our love of money, our yearning for
it, our orienting of our entire lives around the getting of it—
that will bankrupt us.

* Matthew 6:24.

Only later did I discover what to be For instead. I had to learn how to be For the simple act of generosity and wise stewardship. It turned out that generosity wasn't about income level or money management or giving-to-get-back; generosity was a posture for one another and a practice of goodness. For the purposeful practice of freedom from the world's predatory economy to be generous right where we are, with what we have in hand. Wholeness, joy, rest, and openhanded generosity are hallmarks of a life lived within that Jesus-shaped abundance. In fact, mutual giving or sharing is an act of resistance.

Archbishop Desmond Tutu used the Dead Sea as an example of how this works,

> The Dead Sea in the Middle East receives fresh water, but it has no outlet, so it doesn't pass the water out. It receives beautiful water from the rivers, and the water goes dank. I mean, it just goes bad. And that's why it is the Dead Sea. It receives and does not give. In the end generosity is the best way of becoming more, more, and more joyful.[5]

Generosity fights the spirit of greed and the injustice of poverty that have gripped our world. We're learning to be generous and wise in every way from within our real budget-conscious lives. God's abundance is the story we're telling with every corner of our lives, even our bank accounts and spending habits.

So, if I'm For generosity, for giving, for abundance, for equity, then my bank account can reflect that, my choices for spending my money can reflect that, my friendships can reflect that. Do you see? Begin with Against, and keep going until you find your For. It's an act of defiant faith. It will give you something to lean into. It will give you a path to follow.

EMBODIED FOR

The rise of the antiracism movement in 2020 was strong and good, but my wise friend Jeff Chu noted that we needed to remember we're not just against racism, we're also *for* human flourishing. That shift—not just Against, but also For—led us at Evolving Faith to begin to structure measurable, actionable steps we could use internally to look for ways to not only oppose what was broken but also explore ways to cultivate joy, rest, justice, and sanctuary.

Predominantly white spaces, including and sometimes especially, progressive white spaces, can be exhausting for people of color. And so as part of our commitment to human flourishing, Jeff imagined a sanctuary for BIPOC (Black, Indigenous, and People of Color) folks to gather and exhale together. That was the origin of the BIPOC lounge at Evolving Faith: a practical space to rest, laugh, connect, debrief, and exhale. We rented an extra room, hired people with spiritual care experience to hang out there and be available for deeper conversations, brought in food, chairs, and even games. The challenges of an evolving faith are unique for BIPOC folks, and witnessing their repeatedly expressed relief at that simple sanctuary gave us a glimpse of what it meant to be For, not just Against. Dismantling white supremacy has to include looking for ways to cultivate and build an oasis of joy, rest, beauty, and togetherness.

The BIPOC-led space continues to be one of pastoral and relational importance within the community. It's not my space, it isn't supposed to be. Not everything is for everyone. But if we had stopped at simply feeling Against white supremacy—a dominant power and principality in our world—we would have missed how to be For the flourishing of BIPOC folks in a practical, humble, and embodied way.

In my work at the edges of Heartline Ministries in Haiti, I've seen this Against and For manifested in such practical and beautiful ways. Originally established as an orphanage to care for the never-ending stream of children orphaned and made vulnerable by poverty and maternal death in Haiti, Heartline did pretty good work for a long time. They operated as a children's home and served as an adoption facilitator; many Haitian kids were placed into forever families all around the world, but especially in the USA. In addition to the children's home, Heartline established a men's education center, a women's skilled training center, a prison ministry, and countless other programs. Hundreds of churches support orphanages just like this because they are doing real and tangible mission work.

But as the years went by it became more and more obvious that no matter how many children Heartline cared for and placed into families, there were always more motherless and abandoned kids to take their place. It was never-ending.

As Archbishop Desmond Tutu said, "There comes a point where we need to stop pulling people out of the river. We need to go upstream and find out why they're falling in."[6] That is the work of being For things. Heartline decided to look upstream, and what they found was the devastation that poverty-stricken mothers and fathers and families were experiencing because of the relinquishment of their children. Birth control and family planning education were either unavailable or unreliable. Not only did mothers in Haiti lack maternal health support before and after birth, but many were dying in childbirth from preventable and common complications. Even if they survived, the system wasn't set up for a healthy mother-child bond and flourishing.

The women of Haiti wanted their babies, but the system was stacked against them. And part of that system was the adoption-industrial complex that had sprung up, and the way it prioritized the adopting of internationally born kids into American homes rather than fixing the conditions that led to their relinquishment. A lot of kids in orphanages have families, but those families chose to relinquish their children for adoption out of desperation and despair.* As redemptive as adoption is and can be, here it was born out of preventable tragedy and preventable loss.

Heartline began to wonder, what if they turned away from placing children in adoptive homes and turned toward the women and families who were giving up their babies? What if they turned all the energy they were giving to caring for orphans toward making sure that those children never became orphans? Heartline had a hunch that if they cared for and supported expectant women right from the early days of their pregnancy, through delivery, and then afterward—offering everything from education to economic opportunities to medical care—they might not need their orphanage anymore. Heartline wanted their ministries to be For the women of Haiti, to see them thriving and empowered.

Their "For" began with a humble prenatal care program, mainly education and community support, with twenty preg-

---

* The adoption conversation in developing and colonized nations is a complicated and difficult one. Not only do families relinquish children because of death and poverty but they are often preyed upon by people who seek to profit from their pain by "selling" their children to orphanages or adoptive families, often without the knowledge of the adoptive families. The stories are heartbreaking.

nant women. Then in 2010, a horrific earthquake struck Haiti, and everything changed overnight. Like most of the island, Heartline's staff and community was completely devastated, experiencing unimaginable trauma and loss. In the aftermath of the disaster, all of the kids still at the children's home had their adoption visas expedited by the United States, and their new families worked to whisk the children to safety, to their promised new homes. For the first time in years, the Heartline children's home was really and truly empty.

Once the immediate danger and recovery phases passed, and now that they knew what they knew, Heartline couldn't go back to what they did before. Status quo was over. No more Band-Aids on big wounds.

My friend Tara Livesay went back to school to become a midwife at Heartline. At an age when most women are holding steady, she did something incredibly out of her comfort zone and started over. She put in the time, money, energy to become trained, certified, prepared to deliver babies, yes, but also to care for women. Other midwives also trained, and other more well-established midwives came to help.

The children's home remained closed, and instead Heartline opened labor and delivery services. They hired certified nurses from within Haiti. They brought in ob-gyns and midwives from the United States to establish medical protocols and provide support and direction. They hired local residents as caregivers and support staff, employing dozens of Haitians for the new venture. It wasn't perfect. Sometimes things went awry, sometimes Heartline wondered why they were trying so hard to swim upstream. It often felt futile. Impossible. Ridiculous, even. But they kept going, believing that it wasn't enough to just turn away from unwittingly contributing to the orphan crisis. They had to be part of turning toward empowering families in real, practical ways.

Since the establishment of the maternity center, hundreds of babies have been born there. Of those babies, only one has been relinquished for adoption; the rest have remained with their mothers and families of origin. Now Heartline provides prenatal care and classes covering a range of topics, from preparation for delivery to breastfeeding to infant care and attachment.* And they provide delivery on site, where they are equipped to handle most common complications. As a result, their work reduces maternal mortality and infant morbidity rates by a staggering amount.

THERE IS A JEWISH CONCEPT called "tikkun olam" that has caught my imagination, and it might serve you, too. It translates as "healing of the world," and it is considered the work of all of us. We're all called to repair the world. I love this way of seeing things; it gives us work that is sacred, necessary, and daily. It reminds me that everything we do, every choice we make, every life we affect, matters.

We can't save the whole world. We can't fix everything that is broken. There will always be something to be Against here. But the cure for my despair and inaction has been the hope of being For the repair of the world. Rather than just being Against motherless children and full orphanages and underserved women, we get to be For women, for children, for agency, for health. Being For the belief that all women deserve access to quality maternal healthcare, regardless of wealth, race,

---

* They also provide birth control and family planning education.

or faith background. Being For tackling the root causes of poverty, oppression, and injustice in the world by equipping women to support their communities and families. Being For God's dream of shalom, that all-encompassing active peace that is more than the absence of conflict, but is the life-giving presence of justice, wholeness, and flourishing.*

Turn away, yes, but remember to turn toward what you hope for, what you dream for, what you yearn for, too.

Don't miss it. Don't miss the rhythm of justice and healing that your life can sing out right in the face of dominions of despair. Don't miss the invitation hiding there in your Against. Something good is waiting on the other side. If you already know "not this," begin to explore and dream about what could be the alternative. The alternative story, the alternative you, the alternative future, the alternative healing. You might need time to live into it, it might be hard work, it might feel futile and small and ridiculous. And yet there you will be, with a baptized imagination and a dawning sense of what is possible and a ferocious commitment to hope, moving toward Love.

For you,
S.

---

* To check out the full Theology of Care at Heartline, go to heartlineministries .org.

Chapter 15

CHOOSE PEACEMAKING

Dear Accomplice,

I've often been more of a peacekeeper than a peacemaker. I've made the mistake of confusing calmness or the absence of active conflict for peace, of believing disruption is not peaceful behavior, of thinking that if people were just nicer and more polite maybe then the powerful would stop being so terrible. I've acted like avoiding things until they go away was the same thing as being peaceful.*

I'll save you some trouble: this is not peacemaking. This is peacekeeping, which is a stalemate of mediocrity, a status quo maintainer, and sometimes even cooperation with oppression. Yay for me! Peacemaking, on the other hand, brings peace to us, not simply by the absence of conflict, but by reconciliation and the active embodiment of shalom.

This is an area where I have had to turn and face a new direction, over and over again. It's another sacred site of ongoing repentance and transformation for me as I shared earlier. Some of this is my own stuff to deal with, of course, but some of it is the cultural conditioning of femininity, particularly in religion, the high value placed on being "a nice girl" and "easy to get along with." Some of it is Canadianness 101: if someone bumps into me, I will apologize profusely. Basically, I didn't have a

---

* It's cute how I've written this like it's all past tense.

chance. I was always going to think that "going along to get along" is the right choice; I was always going to think it's better to "put up and shut up" than to disrupt.

For people like me, peacemaking is going to be a difficult invitation. I'd be lying if I said I was good at this. To this day, I practice this with gritted teeth and shaky hands. Every hard conversation or confrontation I have is fraught with self-doubt and panicky second-guessing, badly executed attempts and sleepless nights. Basically, this is what I meant when I said that I would be alongside you here in the wilderness, but I probably shouldn't be anyone's guide. Not really.

Do you mind if we start with a story? It's an old one; it might be familiar to you. It involves three siblings—Mary, Martha, and Lazarus—who were all good friends of Jesus.* In this story, Lazarus has fallen ill, so the sisters send word to Jesus: "The one you love so very much is sick." They don't name their brother, instead they say, "The one you love." Can you hear the longing and hope in these simple words?

But Jesus seemingly brushes off the message, telling his disciples that the sickness isn't fatal and that it will actually showcase God's glory. They wait a couple of days, and then Jesus says it's time to go back to Judea. The disciples aren't exactly keen on that idea—there are people there who wish to kill Jesus—but he says he will "wake up" Lazarus. The disciples naturally think he is talking about Lazarus actually sleeping, possibly recovering from his illness, but Jesus knows the truth: Lazarus is already dead. Jesus says to the disciples that he's glad for their sakes that he wasn't in Judea at the time, because something amazing is about to happen.

* John 11:1–44 MSG.

When Jesus finally shows up, Lazarus has been dead for four days. This story becomes a turning point toward the end for Jesus. Because of what is about to happen, Jesus will catch the eye of the powerful in a greater way. From then on, they plot to kill him.

Martha comes out to meet Jesus as he arrives, Mary remains in the house. Think about that detail for a minute. Mary, who during Jesus's earlier visit took the place of a student or a disciple at the feet of her rabbi, Jesus, even though women weren't usually allowed that position. That same Mary, who chose to sit there and listen instead of doing women's traditional work. She remains in the house.

But Martha heads out to Jesus with one question burning on her lips: where were you? "If you'd been here, my brother wouldn't have died," she says. We don't know what her tone was. We don't know if her words were spoken in anger or sorrow, in accusation or wistful longing. Maybe it was a bit of them all. Then she says, "Even now, I know that whatever you ask God he will give you."

Martha is often remembered from the story of Jesus's earlier visit as the "busy one" who failed to choose the "better thing" of sitting at Jesus's feet.* I've never liked that interpretation. Martha isn't the bad guy in that story at all, and it's cartoonish to reduce her relationship with Jesus to one often-misunderstood interaction. This moment showcases her as a woman of great faith and trust, too. She is the woman who seems—without precedent—to believe that Jesus could still *do something* here. What he will do or could do she likely doesn't

* Luke 10:38–42.

know, but surely *something;* Jesus is always up to something. She somehow knows this isn't the end of her brother's story.

Her faith and fierce hope and intelligence invite Jesus to offer her one of his great "I am . . ." statements. Jesus tells Martha that her brother will be raised up, and she has a dutiful right answer ready: yes, of course, "I know that he will be raised up in the resurrection at the end of time."

But Jesus says, "You don't have to wait for the End. I am, right now, Resurrection and Life. The one who believes in me, even though he or she dies, will live. And everyone who lives believing in me does not ultimately die at all."

Hearing this, Martha expresses the same realization that Peter will come to just a little further down the line: "*You are the Messiah, the Son of God.*"

And then of course she runs to get her sister, which would have been my *exact* same reaction.

Mary jumps up and runs toward Jesus. She falls at his feet and, like her sister, says, "If only you had been here, my brother wouldn't have died." In my mind, Martha sounded a bit fierce when she delivered those words; Mary sounds heartbroken. She sobs at his feet and, rather than responding to her the way he did to Martha, Jesus answers with his own emotion, becoming angry—angry at death, at sickness, at the grave. He demands to know where Lazarus has been entombed, and when they tell him, he weeps.

Jesus wept.

The text doesn't tell us much beyond these powerful two words, but much has been made of them. Even if all is redeemed, even if Jesus fully knew what he would do here, even if there is a theological argument and a miracle pending, Jesus responds to the tears of Mary and the grief of their community with his own tears. As Cole Arthur Riley writes, "You can't tell me that it doesn't change everything that the one who created all things and holds together all things cried."[1]

At the sight of his tears, some remark on how deeply Jesus had loved Lazarus, but others begin to whisper, "Well, if he loved him so much, why didn't he do something to keep him from dying?" Jesus and the disciples continue to the tomb, but Jesus is still angry: when they arrive, he says, "Remove the stone."

Martha, ever-practical and ever-unafraid of telling the truth, even to the Messiah, says that if they remove the stone, the stench of the rotting body will be horrible. After all, Lazarus has been dead four days. We needn't pretend this is pleasant, Jesus. But Jesus looks her straight in the eye and says, "Didn't I tell you that if you believed, you would see the glory of God?" The text doesn't tell us what she said in response, but Jesus's next demand for the stone to be removed is met with no opposition, no arguments. I imagine the people looking to Martha for permission to roll away that stone before they begin. I imagine her weighing what she knows in her heart with what she knows in her mind, looking at Jesus, looking at that stone, and simply nodding. *Do what he says.*

Jesus then prays aloud for the benefit of the crowd gathered around, and he hollers, "Lazarus! Come out!" And out of the grave walks Lazarus, still wrapped up in his graveclothes from head to toe, even the kerchief is still covering his face.

Then comes an often unremarked and yet remarkable statement from Jesus. He tells Mary and Martha and the crowd, "Unwrap him and let him loose." Some translations use the phrase "unbind him." Lazarus has been raised from the dead,

but he is still bound by the clothes of the dead. He's still en-
cased in the remnants of death. It will take the hands of his
sisters and his friends to unbind him, to set him loose to life
again.

With those words, Jesus invites the community—us—into
the work of resurrection.

THE MIRACLE INCLUDES US

The dead have risen, now we are part of the unbinding. We are
called to unbind what was bound in death. The miracle doesn't
exclude us, it includes us.

I keep seeing this baffling and life-changing moment over
and over again in Jesus's miracles and signs of the kin-dom: the
moment of invitation to participate.

We are always invited to be in on what God is doing among
us and to be part of the new way of life.

Look at the miraculous feedings of four thousand and five
thousand in the book of Mark.* Both times, Jesus asks the disciples what they have—it is, of course, never enough. And each
time Jesus blesses what they have, breaks it, and then gives it
back to them. They are invited to participate in the feeding.
The miracle isn't only in the multiplying; the miracle unfolds in
the *invitation to participate*. The miracle also happens because
someone brings five or seven loaves of bread and a few fish. The
miracle also happens because the disciples hand out the food to
the crowd.

We perhaps see this most clearly at the ascension of Jesus
himself. He commissions the disciples—in that moment and

---

* Mark 6:35–44, 8:14–21.

for all of time. Likewise, he invites us to continually *participate* in this new life by saying, "All authority in heaven and on earth has been given to me. Therefore go and make disciples of all nations, baptizing them in the name of the Father and of the Son and of the Holy Spirit, and teaching them to obey everything I have commanded you. And surely I am with you always, to the very end of the age."*

There is always an invitation to participate in the unbinding of what was dead and is now alive, an invitation to participate in the feeding, an invitation to participate in the life of the Christ now. Unlike peacekeeping, peacemaking requires participation.

And yes, I still believe the Spirit is at work at this moment. But the work of the Spirit is never an excuse for inaction or silence: it is actually the very invitation to participate in the unbinding, the feeding, the healing, the tearing down and building up.

Now we have work to do.

Now we are commissioned in the resurrection life.

Now we unwind the graveclothes because we are called to justice.

It's one thing for us to sing resurrection songs or offer platitudes at funerals about how this isn't the end or blandly imply that there isn't anything we can do because racism or systemic injustice or white supremacy is really just a heart issue, too bad. It's another thing entirely to believe that our practice of resurrection has implications for the hungry, for the bound, for the oppressed, for the marginalized, for the silenced, for the dead among us.

* Matthew 28:18–20, NIV.

This is why I see such a beautiful invitation toward participation in resurrection for us now. It's an invitation to that active and embodied peacemaking. It's an invitation to rip the graveclothes right off and pass out bread to the hungry and tear down structures that oppress.

We're on the same side as Love now. Walter Brueggemann writes,

> The vision of wholeness, which is the supreme will of the biblical God, is the outgrowth of a covenant of shalom, in which persons are bound not only to God but to one another in a caring, sharing, rejoicing community with none to make them afraid.[2]

This is the difference between peacemaking and peacekeeping, I believe. Peacekeeping says, "It will stink if you open the door, let what is dead stay dead."

Peace*making* not only says, "Remove the stone!" and "Lazarus, come out!" but also says, "Unbind him from the clothing of the dead," and then gets to work.

I HATE THE WORK, BUT IT WORKS

A number of years ago, I started a new physical rehabilitation program in addition to a whole host of shifts in caring for my body. I had been injured in a car accident, and it proved to be a long road of imperfect healing, including a fibromyalgia diagnosis, a broken foot, chronic pain, and other fun things.[*] At about the time I was hitting rock bottom physically and emo-

---

* If you're interested, you can read more about my car accident and how the story unfolded in *Miracles and Other Reasonable Things*.

tionally, I was cleared to begin this new rehab program, and so it began.

My friend Megan is a kinesiologist, and it was to her facility I dragged myself. I went through assessments and agreements, then began to show up multiple times a week to a small storefront on the main street of our town to do exercises, lift tiny weights, move my stubborn body, and be encouraged by my therapists. They were intent on increasing my mobility and strength, figuring out triggers, as well as managing symptoms and learning how to get in front of my pain. They were incredibly kind and warm, professional and knowledgeable. The little center mainly served older folks, who were twice as strong as I was if not quite that much older, and they were always incredibly encouraging of my attempts.

Oh, and one other thing; I hated it with my whole heart.

I do mean that. Hate, hate, hate. For a while, there wasn't a single time I showed up that I hadn't spent the whole drive there wishing I had canceled my appointment. The first time I went for initial assessments and a training session, I cried quietly the entire way through, and by the end, I ran out of the facility in no-longer-quiet tears. I cried in my shower for almost an hour after most sessions, multiple times.* There were a lot of reasons: some of it was the actual physical exertion of moving muscles and joints that had been damaged. It could take me a day or two to recover from a session. But a lot of it was also frustration, grief, even anger and humiliation. It was some of the hardest work I had ever done—and I am someone who has given birth to four half-Nebraskan babies.

Don't misunderstand me: I was under the care of a team of

---

* Pro tip: showers are great places for crying!

experts, and the exercises that I was doing in the beginning made the octogenarians at the pool doing gentle water yoga look like elite athletes. The things I did in that program would have looked inconsequential to outside eyes. My therapist would demonstrate some seemingly small thing: "Here, you are going to stand at this wall and rotate your hip joint." "Easy, got it," I'd reply. Until I tried it and was left clinging to the wall after three rotations, cursing the sun, moon, and stars in expletives I didn't even know I knew. This program was humbling and sweaty and impossible. I resented every minute.

AND HERE'S THE WORST PART: it worked. It did.

I know, I hate that, too.

The exercise that made me cry in the shower at the beginning? I could do eighteen repetitions of that exercise six weeks later. Eighteen! I began to get stronger. The program helped me to cope and manage pain and flare-up days much better, too. I grew more resilient, and those small things added up.

I came away from this experience realizing that the work that is mine to do, I need to be faithful to do.

I hate these sorts of metaphors. I know they are true, and that makes me resent them even more. I wish we could wave magic wands to heal and I wish that every prayer was instantly answered and I wish I wish I wish. I wish that wishing worked half as well as plain work.

But the invitation is to the work. And it's at that intersection of showing up and doing the work that transformation happens.

That first terrible week, I called my sister (crying, of course), and she very gently said, "You always had to start somewhere.

And if you keep going, you will get stronger. So keep going." And so I did.

I think that's why I've been drawn to that little detail of unwinding the graveclothes as part of peacemaking. The work of our time is to look at the valleys of inequity and oppression and raise them up, to dismantle the mountains of privilege, to make the rugged places of struggle and inequality and poverty and pain into a wide place of rest for everyone.*

I keep seeing this baffling and life-changing moment over and over again in Jesus's ministry: this invitation to participate in the peacemaking, in the embodiment of the ways of shalom, the kin-dom of God on earth as it is in heaven, in tearing down mountains and making the paths straight.

The wilderness has a way of stripping polite peacekeeping away from us in the end. We see it for the anemic bet-hedging prop that it is at heart. Peacekeeping says, "The mountains have always been there." Peace*making* says, "Let's cast this mountain into the sea" and "Make the way straight" and it also gets to the work of disrupting and dismantling and liberating to actively embody the covenant of shalom for all people.

bell hooks writes,

> dominator culture has tried to keep us all afraid, to make us choose safety instead of risk, sameness instead of diversity. Moving through that fear, finding out what connects us, reveling in our differences; this is the process that brings us closer, that gives us a world of shared values, of meaningful community.[3]

---

* Isaiah 40:4.

Learning to practice meaningful peacemaking in community has been uncomfortable and hard and also the best work I'll probably have to keep doing the rest of my life.

One of the things I hope for you is that your own experience here in the wilderness will not be only for you. Of course I hope that your time here, your own paths and invitations, brings peace to you, but also to those around you.

Every day we show up to do it, we repair the world just a bit more. Much like my rehab program, which started with small work, seemingly ridiculous and repetitive work, peacemaking can begin in humble, sweaty, uncomfortable ways. It can begin with a lot of crying in the shower. It can be frustrating, and you might get uncomfortable. Keep going.

The invitation of peacemaking is always present to us. We're learning to make the rooms of our own hearts ready for hope and for peace. We try to remember to pray for our enemies and to love our neighbors and to practice these ways of Jesus as if he meant them—because I have a hunch he did mean them. Even if we don't know what we believe about any of it yet, there is still good work to do while we figure it out, isn't there?

We won't choose silence and despair and the litany of numb anger anymore. When we fail—because let's not kid ourselves, we will fail each other and ourselves, we'll make mistakes and get called out, we'll need to get very familiar with humility—we will brush the dust from our faces and the tears from our eyes, we will learn how to start over and over and over.

We will look fear in the face and speak up anyway. We will look hopelessness in the face and declare the hope of the Lord for the redemption and rescue and renewal of all things. We will put ourselves into real work, however humble and imperfect, finding the gift of doing things, of making things, of creating things, of healing things, of feeding people, of bringing order out of chaos even in small ways.

We'll make coffee in the morning and hot meals to gather around the table at suppertime. We'll learn to love what our teenagers love and read good books. We'll pray for our enemies and write letters and send money and fold clothes and drop off meals with an extra bag of groceries. We'll advocate with the marginalized and amplify the oppressed and antagonize the Empire with grins on our faces. We will grab hold of the small scrap of life we have within reach, and there, we'll choose hope. We'll learn how to listen to those with whom we disagree. We will stand in the middle of an open field with our faces turned up to the rain and consider it baptism.

Doing the work isn't always the sexy world-changing thing we think it is, is it? And yet it's always our invitation. The world—even just our small patch of it—is repaired for just one small moment. And I believe with all of my heart, this matters. Part of the work right now is to clearly discern our work and then to simply do it faithfully—or at least stubbornly. Some things are beyond us, some things are not ours to do. But when they are, well, we can be faithful to that good work. We won't settle for peacekeeping or for despair. We'll keep trying to repair the world, to unwind the graveclothes, to pass another bite to someone else who is as hungry as we were.

And as I learned all over again while in that rehab program and ever afterward, showing up and doing the work does change things. Even if you have to cry in the shower sometimes, too.

We always had to start somewhere,
S.

Chapter 16

YOU HAVE PERMISSION
TO BE HAPPY

Dear Courageous One,

Little-known fact: I'm actually a marketer by trade and training. Yep. I studied marketing and communications for my undergraduate degree, and then I spent about twelve years working in the field for financial institutions and nonprofit organizations. My specialty became strategic planning, brand development, and communications. I do still love a good spreadsheet.

I often extolled the virtues of "branding" for organizations. People usually thought "the brand" meant the logo, or perhaps the color scheme, even the look and feel of a company's marketing materials. But really, brand is so much bigger than that. It is the story an organization tells not only through their marketing materials but through their customer service, strategic planning, products, design, and website. Everything a company does tells a story about themselves to the world.

Since my marketing career days, it's become clear to me that the notion of being on-brand isn't exclusive to corporations or nonprofits. We often embrace a certain "brand" for ourselves. We have a story we want to tell with our lives, and we expect everything—our food, our church, our budget, our homes, our friends, our causes, our habits, our choices, our clothes—to reinforce that story. Influencers on social media are often over-realized versions of personal branding. This isn't necessarily negative, but it can be restrictive. Whether we're influencers or not, many of us are unconsciously thinking of what our choices communicate to the world about who we are and what we value and what our purpose is in this life.

My training taught me: Don't disrupt the brand. Don't lose sight of the brand. Don't let go of your brand. And many of our religious environments are a form of branding, too, so we are taught "don't disrupt the brand" in a context of faith and religion.

But sometimes the story we tell ourselves about our own lives can become a prison. Our "brand" can keep us from the real life that is waiting for us.

That's why going off-brand can be terrifying. Daring to change our story when we find our primary identity in that particular story feels like we are losing our own sense of self. It's more than just changing an opinion or a way of life, it's changing who we thought we were.

I always go to this church: but then you find yourself leaving it.

I always believed that being gay was sinful: but then you finally came out and you encountered the love of God in ways you couldn't have imagined when you were denying how God made you.

I always knew I would live in this town for my entire life: but then you find yourself moving away to a new city.

I was raised in a certain political persuasion: but then you find yourself feeling alienated and disoriented, even betrayed, by your political family.

I always knew that marriage was important to me, and I judged people who got divorced: but then you find yourself signing those papers, and underneath the grief, there is an odd and persistent feeling of relief.

I always knew I was called to ministry: but then you find yourself in a regular sort of job, and you have to figure out a new story and deconstruct all those hero narratives you ingested about ministry.

I always knew I would get married and have kids: but then you find yourself single.

I always knew I didn't want to have kids: but then you find yourself with a houseful of small humanity to care for.

I always believed I was in control of my drinking: but now you're hiding your empty bottles from people who love you.

I expected to parent in a particular way: but your kid requires something different and you are having to reimagine a whole new way to raise a child.

I have always encountered God in this one way: but then that way becomes barren and empty and you find yourself walking new paths, as a new seeker of God.

I always thought that I would be one sort of person: but now I'm someone else.

And you've never been more grateful.

YOU DON'T NEED PERMISSION TO go off-brand, but in case you're looking for it, here it is: you have permission to go off-brand. You have permission to change. You have permission, as Parker Palmer said, to "let your life speak" and adjust accordingly.[1]

Further, you have permission to experience joy and gratitude, freedom and wholeness. You have permission to be happy.

Speaker and author Angela Williams Gorrell writes, "Not

only do we need permission to be honest about emotions like sadness, anger, and fear, we need permission to be joy-filled. And we need this permission from other people and ourselves. We can give one another and ourselves permission to experience joy in many ways."[2]

You don't really need my permission to feel joy either, but just in case, here you go: you are allowed to feel joy. And your experience out here in the wilderness is one way you've chosen joy. Communally, personally, in every way, you are choosing joy.

Very early in the pandemic, I came across this poem called "Don't Hesitate," by one of my favorite poets, Mary Oliver, and it has come to mean a lot to me:

If you suddenly and unexpectedly feel joy,
don't hesitate. Give in to it. There are plenty
of lives and whole towns destroyed or about
to be. We are not wise, and not very often
kind. And much can never be redeemed.
Still, life has some possibility left. Perhaps this
is its way of fighting back, that sometimes
something happens better than all the riches
or power in the world. It could be anything,
but very likely you notice it in the instant
when love begins. Anyway, that's often the
case. Anyway, whatever it is, don't be afraid
of its plenty. Joy is not made to be a crumb.

When you're here in the wilderness, your joy isn't made to be a crumb. It can be a whole feast now. Don't mistake despair for holiness in these days. Make friends with your grief so that through the prism of your tears, you can be free to feel the true realities of joy breaking through, undergirding, holding you up, too. Joy is as real as suffering. Love begins, again and again.

When it comes to this experience of an evolving faith, I've come to find it peculiar that we don't talk more about its joy and gratitude. It's not easy to evolve, but oh, there is joy here, too. That's because there is so much being healed, restored, renewed in us.

Granted, the notion of "choosing joy" can be a complicated one for those of us who came up through church cultures where happiness was viewed with distrust. Both overt and covert messages conspired to make us suspicious of joy, like it was a selfish thing. Leftovers from our Puritan roots, perhaps, but somehow we picked up the notion that pursuing joy is a form of selfishness.

Yet joy brings goodness to the world. Research shows that joyful people aren't selfish, in fact they are "more, not less likely, to volunteer their time, donate their money, and help others. The relationship between these prosocial behaviours and happiness could not be explained by how much money people made, or by their gender, age, or religiosity."[3] There are gifts to be gained by everyone around you when you're simply, actually joyful, too.

EMBRACING GRATITUDE AS A PATH TO JOY

In all of my study and conversations with people, it's become abundantly clear that the most grateful people are often the most joyful. It's not that they are dishonest or spiritually bypassing real human emotion. It's that their gratitude, their humility, their generosity have an outlet and it brings them joy.

One of the surprising gifts of embracing lament and truth-telling in my life has been the reclamation of happiness and gratitude that accompanied it. Brené Brown is just preaching truth when she writes, "There is a full spectrum of human emotions and when we numb the dark, we numb the light."[4] Because the wilderness has helped us become more acquainted with grief and loss, it has also given us the pathway back toward joy and gratitude. You will feel it all again.

In fact, everything you're learning out here in the wilderness is leading you toward gratitude and joy again. And, if we want to experience more joy, we need to cultivate our practice of gratitude. It's not a matter of our feelings, although those matter; it's about telling the truth to ourselves, too. It's about embedding practices of joyfulness and thankfulness into our daily life because these deserve your time, energy, and focus, too.

Look for ways to practice gratitude in your life. For a while there, I kept a little notebook at my bedside, and before I turned out the light, I wrote down five things I was grateful for in a bullet point list. Nothing fancy, nothing magic, just: I'm grateful for Evelynn's freckles, I'm grateful for how much Joe loves Simon & Garfunkel albums, I'm grateful for the way Anne invited Maggie to work on a puzzle with her, I'm grateful for Brian's job, I'm grateful for Jeff's text message today. Night after night, I took time to write it down, and day after day, I became more observant, more watchful for gratitude, and even, dare I say, more joyful because of it. Benedictine Brother David Steindl-Rast writes that "the root of joy is gratefulness . . . it is not joy that makes us grateful; it is gratitude that makes us joyful."[5]

Some of us were taught that the only way to be happy and holy was to be an evangelical Christian in a particular church in a particular way, like it was a formula, and a tight one at that. But that isn't true, is it? There are so many ways to be happy and to be holy. There are so many ways to find joy and humility and courage. But because that was the teaching, or perhaps what we most ardently believed or even experienced ourselves for a time, we can feel this need to apologize for our growth and change.

You don't need to apologize for going off-brand. You certainly don't owe anyone an apology for leaving places and people who hurt you or your children or hurt other people you love. You don't need to apologize for your newfound joy. You don't need to apologize for the ways you're waking up to God's good love and wide embrace. You don't need to apologize for where your borders are falling and your heart is expanding.

HAVE FUN ON PURPOSE

One beautiful way to be joyful is to reclaim playfulness, celebration, and fun. Let go of perfectionism. Remember how to have hobbies that don't make you money. Stop trying to monetize what you love, just enjoy it. Paint terrible pictures. Write bad poetry. Knit misshapen things just for yourself. Journal through the experience and then burn that journal in a bonfire. Write songs. Go to karaoke night. Take up softball again. Go out dancing. Learn to play board games online with people around the world. Listen to live music. Plant herbs in old, rinsed-out sour cream containers.

I hope you remember how to play again. If there is some form of creativity that you lost along the way, I hope you rediscover it. If there is something you've always wanted to try, I hope you try it.

In our house, we call this "having fun on purpose." Not everything has to have a big theological reason for being. Sometimes the reason is just that you like it and you have fun doing it.

AFTER THE EVOLVING FAITH CONFERENCE in Atlanta one year, Brian and I decided to fly home out of Nashville. We had worked hard on the event for weeks, so a long drive and a day off to spend in Music City USA sounded good to us. We bought tickets to see Jason Isbell in concert at the Ryman Auditorium, the mother church of country music. Jason Isbell is Brian's favorite singer-songwriter, and I'm a previously established geek for country music going way back to the Ryman's glory days, so this was a perfect storm of fun for us, complete with guided tours and cheesy photographs.

That night, in the balcony of the old auditorium, sitting on generations-old wooden pews worn smooth, we clasped hands and listened to music with our whole bodies. When Jason sang the lines "You thought God was an architect, now you know, he's something like a pipe bomb ready to blow,"[6] I hollered like he was preaching good. When the lady beside us—most certainly of our parents' generation—dressed in her Sunday best and seemingly the bearer of deep Southern-lady sensibilities bellowed the line "I don't wanna die in a Super 8 motel"* with her whole chest, I was more delighted than I've ever been.[7] We sang, clapped, cried. When the concert ended, it felt like Brian and I had been in church.

Maybe we thought that traditional church was the only

---

* The song is called, of course, "Super 8."

source of that kind of connection, but that night we relearned it's a human experience, not restricted to one place or people. Be open to these sorts of transcendent experiences in your life, however you find them, especially in times of evolution.

As author Susan Cain relates, "It's precisely during such times—including career changes, divorces, and the ultimate transition of death—that we're more likely to experience meaning, communion, and transcendence."[8] These collective moments can be signposts, new ways of finding meaning and connection, when your old pathways are unrecognizable. They are the small stitches in our broken hearts, mending us and giving us hope. Right now, right when you're grieving your losses, your heart is perhaps most open to transcendence and connection. Isn't that a wonder?

JOY IS ALSO REAL

One of the many reasons why I still love to mark the turning of our days with the Church's calendar—like for Advent, Lent, or the blessedly named Ordinary Time—is that this rhythm takes a long view of time through birth and life and death, pandemics and boycotts of Disneyland. The Church before us and with us and likely after us will always find themselves at their own moment in time, wondering *how can we talk about joy these days?*, as if having a hard time and the world being a dumpster fire is a brand-new experience. Of course it's not, every generation relearns the Ecclesiastical truth that there is nothing new under the sun.* Right here, in your wilderness, you have an invitation to wild, off-brand, out-of-order joy.

* Ecclesiastes 1:9.

Joy is never intellectually or emotionally or spiritually dis-honest. It certainly isn't more doubling down on "it's fine, we're fine, everything is fine" when things are clearly and obviously not fine. Joy isn't a good time earned through denial or perfor-mative sentimentality or spiritual bypassing.

No one feels happy all the time. That's ludicrous and imma-ture to expect or demand of ourselves, then or now. You're a person, luv. You're going to have days when you're sad and lonely, misunderstood and longing. And you'll have days of joy and transcendence. Nothing about the human experience lasts forever. Sometimes this is terrifying, but it becomes a comfort.

One of the great free joys of the Gospel's reality is Jesus mov-ing toward the margins to redraw the center of God's geometry there. God making a home among the unwanteds, eating with the overlooked. Again, the Gospel isn't only for the wealthy or influential or powerful: look at the people God chose. People who were poor, distrusted, ostracized, sick, old, sex workers, tax collectors, women, illiterate peasants, fishermen, prosper-ous businesswomen, folks from the wrong side of the tracks—us! Us! Ours is the kin-dom of God, too. Ah, such good news, eh?

These moments of joy aren't erasing reality; the joy is just part of the reality, too. It isn't only sad and tragic things that are real: redemption is real, renewal is real, joy is still real. Kisses in the kitchen and underlined poems and herons gliding low over the water are real. Nurses who stand vigil at bedsides and teach-ers who read stories aloud and sanitation workers who dress up as superheroes to collect trash so that kids stuck inside sick have something to look forward to while the days pass, all real. Eucharist and old hymns, iron-gray skies and hearing the words "I love you still" are real, too. A Savior who sits in our sorrow, lentil soup simmering on the stove, forgiveness, all real.

Our suffering and sadness don't make our newfound joy un-
true. Our suffering and our sadness mean that these are the
very days for the prophetic resistance of your joy, for the practice and discipline of joy, for the truth of joy right in the teeth
of despair.

CELEBRATE AND IMPROVISE

My friend Kathy Escobar co-pastors a church in Colorado
called The Refuge. Their tagline is "Throwing parties, sharing
stories, finding hope, practicing the ways of Jesus as best as we
can." In her book *Practicing,* Kathy writes about their church's
stubborn insistence on celebration, giving parties for everything from sobriety anniversaries to new babies. "Every positive movement in the human experience is worth celebrating.
In a world that's hard and in need of tender loving care, we
sometimes miss the practice of celebrating. We become so focused on what *isn't* that we forget the good that *is.* We forget to
make time and space for parties and other celebrations and
honor the diverse and wonderful way we are all transforming."[9]

Your transformations are worth celebrating. Maybe you
should throw a party. Or, if you're an introvert like me who
thinks parties that last beyond 9:00 P.M. are abominations unto
the Lord, maybe go for a nice solitary walk or write a bit in
your journal or find some way to celebrate and bless your own
transformations. You are worth celebrating. Rituals to create
meaning aren't just for our sorrows and losses. Celebrate a
month without booze, celebrate a new job, celebrate your tiny
little apartment, where you're living alone for the first time
ever, celebrate your kid's faithfulness to show up for math tu-
toring; celebrate babies and marriages, sure, but celebrate sin-

gleness and friendship, too. Become embedded in your life, in your neighborhood, in your community until everything that is ordinary becomes beautiful and worthy of praise to you.

YES, AND . . .

I don't recall much from the improv class I took in junior high,[10] but I will always remember the phrase "yes, and." If you were in an improv with someone else and they said something—anything—your job as their improv partner was to respond "Yes, and . . ." However wild and outrageous and unexpected your partner acted, you said, "Yes, *and . . .*" because you needed to keep the performance going by picking up where your partner left off. You were supposed to "yes, and" in your language and your body and your spirit in order to keep the energy flowing and the performance moving and to even create art. (Which feels like very high expectations for a junior high drama class, but this is why we love teachers.) Whatever happened in that session, your main job was to respond with open arms and a spirit of possibility. Every improv will be different because you're there and the other person is there and the audience is there and the energy changes.

I think of our journey in that sort of improvisational way now. This is an off-brand altar of "yes, and."

Yes, I've changed. And I still belong.

Yes, I have questions. And I still belong.

Yes, I used to think one thing and now I live something different. And I still belong.

Yes, my relationship with religion is best described as "it's complicated" right now. And I still belong.

Yes, I'm hurting and wounded and I have hurt and I have wounded. And I still belong.

Yes, I am filled with doubt and disbelief and wonder at the same time. And I still belong.

Yes, I don't know what I think about really any of this. And I still belong.

Yes, I'm trying to figure out what it means to love God and love people well. And I still belong.

Yes, I'm anxious and scared. Yes, I'm sad and I'm lonesome. And I still belong.

Yes, I don't even know how or what to ask and yet I will still receive.

IF ALL YOU'VE DONE IS traded one tired script for a new one, you've missed the improvisation of the Spirit. You're not a brand, beloved. On this journey you'll lose your scripts again and again. Life will happen. Your heart will be broken. You'll be disappointed again. You will run out of answers again. You will think you've nailed your lines and then you'll hear, "But what about . . ." and once again, you'll begin again.

The poet and musician Peter Riley calls the improvision during live music performances the "exploration of the occasion." I think that's part of what we're doing now in the wilderness. Your life is an exploration of the occasion. We're improvising, not out of disrespect, let alone a desire for sin and license or even out of fury, but out of exploration and questioning and the possibility for love. There is freedom to improvise even if there are some similarities, helpful scaffolding, shared language, rituals, and sacraments to hold us up as we grow bolder and more loving. Your life was never meant to be a brand. It was always an exploration of love and life.

Life and spirituality will be different in the wilderness this time—as compared to every time you've done this before—because you're different. This moment in time is different. This place is different. Your life is different. You are in the exploration of the occasion. And that's as it should be. An evolving faith is always a remix.

You're in a new place and a new way because of your wanderings and wonderings, your doubts and possibilities, your healing and your hope, let alone the larger stories of your community and your people and your place. You have been working so hard to love others in a way that you yourself were not loved. You are seeking justice after being treated unjustly. You're turning your own loss and pain into a shelter for others. You glorious resurrection story, you.

It takes such holy audacity to choose a new path when the old ways turn into dead ends for you. It takes guts to realize that God is bigger than a church, a tradition, an interpretation, and then to live accordingly.

Yes, you have songs you still love and the prayers you rest in and the candles you light and the lines from Isaiah that still come to your lips. Yes, the real Jesus you're still meeting for the first time over and over somehow still feels like a friend and the one who makes sense in the midst of all this. And it will make you glad.

We are learning to receive, not control. We are learning to improvise, to play again, and to reclaim our joy. I'm thinking of you tearing up your scripts and tossing the pieces into the fire and whooping under the full moon. Because you still cherish the Sunday school teacher who hugged you tight every week and the friend who stayed by your side during chemo and the teacher who came along at the right time for you, and the prayers of your grandmothers, the hymns that somehow are the ones you hum late at night when you think no one hears you, and the way you still want to say "thank you" when you see the sun set into the horizon, leaving only streaks of light across a navy sky. The knowing in your heart that love is enough of an answer and even the possibility of joy is enough to say, "Yes, and . . ."

I think you make God happy,
S.

Chapter 17

NOW WE'RE JUST GETTING STARTED

Dear Companion,

A couple of years ago, I happened across an article in *Smith-sonian* magazine about a small Christmas tree farm in Massa-chusetts. Not my usual fare, I admit, but something about the story caught my eye and it has stayed with me ever since. Be-cause instead of the neat rows of fat, snug trees, the use of fertil-izers or insecticides, and the typical rhythm of cutting down trees, digging up the roots, and then planting a brand-new tree in that spot just to do it all over again, this family farm does something different. They cultivate the stumps of older trees to grow their new trees.[1]

Picture a whole forest of old tree stumps, all growing new, thriving trees, over and over again. These natural Christmas trees are equal parts wild and cultivated, untamed and tradi-tional. A tree hardly ever dies in this forest; it is simply har-vested well, and the original stump continues reproducing over and over again with the cooperation of gardener, land, nature, and science.

It is a method called "coppicing." When the farmer harvests the original tree, he makes the cut higher up the trunk so the stump and the roots remain alive, creating the foundation for all the trees that will be grown in the future. And because the stump has to be cut higher up the tree, the sunlight can reach the forest floor, bringing greater ecological diversity and health to the whole forest, old and new mingled together. The farm featured in the story was situated on land that was rocky and steep, so even if they wanted to farm it in the conventional way, the terrain wouldn't allow it. Instead they cooperate with the land.

Maybe, a while ago, a minute ago, we would have looked out into this wilderness and imagined only danger. Perhaps our hopeless eyes still see a barren forest of tree stumps, but gardeners who remember the ancient paths? They see the possibilities of new life. And not new life as it was before—no, that's over, and pretending otherwise does no one any favors. Ours is a defiant new life born out of the roots of what was cut away, from what most folks would dismiss as over and done. This is a tender beginning that grows with room to breathe, a wild tang in the air, the song of the sunlight reaching all the way to the mosses under your feet, with irregular beauty and space to stretch out your boughs at last.

For some of us, it's hard to accept that your new life is here now. There isn't a "there" to go back to, not anymore. And at this point in your journey, as you gather your things and prepare to head out, I want to tell you that the aspects of your story some people want to "fix" for you? Those are the very things that are fixing everything. Claim your whole story. All of your life belongs to you. You might be surprised by the unexpected harvest of this.

Me? I do want the moments of joy: the moments when my children came into the world, when I saw Brian waiting for me at the end of a chapel aisle in Tulsa, when I dove into the cold lake water as a kid, when I slept across from my sister for years, when I held my first published book in my hands. I want the joy and peace I have felt in church, in prayer, in ordinary walks in the woods. I want the moment I stood alone on the cliff on Prince Edward Island and was introduced all over again to the sweep of the Holy Spirit's wind and bright joy. I want every late-night snuggle and *Doctor Who* episode* and early morning coffee. I want obnoxious waterslides and solitary trails through prairie grass and sleepovers with cousins.

And I also want those moments of pain and sorrow now. I want the regrets I have had to grapple with, the sin I have had to repent of; I want the night we lay on the floor after yet another loss of a baby, crying so hard that it felt like we were underwater because the tears had pooled in our ears. I want the unanswered prayers, the failures. I even want my car accident, the painful recovery, the reduced strength and ability that I still experience, because it has profoundly changed my soul to be on the slower, painful, losing side of the path. I want the mistakes, the judgments, the misunderstandings. I want the churches that broke my heart, the friends who have betrayed or simply forgotten me. I want the things I learned from hard experiences I wouldn't repeat for a million dollars. I want the waves of grief: it means I knew love and friendship well. I want the scars I carry, visible and invisible. I earned every single one.

I have needed my strengths and my faults, my victories and my sorrows, altogether. Their totality is the spiritual formation of being a person in this world. We aren't meant to be untouched or unmoved or unchanged by living. I wouldn't trade a moment of what brought me here, not now. Like the old trees bearing new life, I am the sum total of all those moments— without the suffering, without the sorrow, I would miss the ordinary joy of living right now in this blessed body.

* Fine, I could probably do without "Love & Monsters."

The parts of myself that I would have wanted to fix or erase in my teens and twenties and even into my thirties (fine, mid-forties)—I see these are the gifts now (most of the time). I wouldn't be the woman, the wife, the mother, the friend, the writer, the disciple of Jesus I am today without my faults and my sorrows any more than without my strengths and my joys. That's not to say that I wallow in my faults, but they are often invitations to truth, belonging, and plain humility. This wholeness, this full belonging of everything, is what makes me able to love and to live. I have a hunch that you'd say the same thing about your own whole life.

This doesn't undo what stole your hope from you, beloved: this is hope that kisses your wounds, gently binds up your broken heart, and breathes new life into the parts of you that you think are dead and then attends to you until the deep knowing of the Love that holds all of us takes root again. This Gardener of hope sees the root of life still in you and cultivates everything that is wild and unexpected, hopeful and redemptive in you, bringing forth life you never imagined, a life that repairs the world at your feet.

The old hopes are there even as new hope develops and then flourishes; we could not have one without the other. The hope we have is built on nothing less.

Makeshift Tables in the Wilderness

Not long ago I was preaching in the Midwest, to a community where I counted many of the folks as friends. One thing that always struck me about their church was their setup; rather than rows facing a stage, they arranged the chairs in a circle around a giant table, topped with baskets of bread and carafes of wine, lit by candles, decorated with natural elements from the season. The song leader sat to the side of it; when I preached, I was on the other side. The Table was the focal point; the Eucharist was more central to their gathering than my sermon or the songs we would sing together. Their formation as a community was as a circle, not a stage.

On that particular evening, we had filled the round chapel with our songs and with our prayers. We sang like a choir would sing: loud and big, right to the rafters together, as if we meant every word in that moment. I know I did. I still do, to be honest, most days.

The candles flickered, and then I stood up to proclaim the power of the resurrection in my own life, how resurrection crept in slowly like the spring, and how every place of death and barrenness in my life was renewed, not in spite of a faith shift but because of it. An evolving faith has given room for flowers to grow and wild vines to take root in my life. Much like those coppiced trees, it has brought ecological diversity and flourishing, too.

After I took my seat, the church stood up together. At each of the four corners of the Table, two people stepped forward to serve as ministers of the Eucharist. One held the bread, one held the wine. The church quietly filed up to the Table, and as each person approached a server, they cupped their hands together to receive the bread without grasping for it. As they received the bread and wine, I could hear the ministers say each person's name along with "This is the Body of Christ broken for you, this is the blood of Christ poured out for you." Over and over, until everyone had bread and everyone had wine. Here was the Table, open, *come as you are.*

We live in the Kin-dom of God, or what theologians call

"Now and Not Yet," of God's goodness at this moment in time and space. Sometimes it feels like there are so many, too many, things that are still "not yet." We're not yet at farming over fighting, we're not yet at swords into plowshares, we're not yet at no more sorrow, no more pain, no more injustice. We're not yet at the lion and the lamb lying down together, we're not yet seeing all of our deserts bloom and our brokenness made whole.*

But sometimes I can forget that there is still power for now, too. Wonder-working power even, power here in these imperfect gatherings with imperfect people with imperfect theology who dare to believe that God's heart is for us, God's dream for us is wholeness and shalom and redemption. Maybe the power of God is most made manifest in our "Not Yet" moments simply because we're not alone, not anymore. God has come to us then and now and always. And even then, we are together. Even here, out here, in the wilderness.

ON THAT EVENING AND IN that church, I went forward to receive communion. I have done this thousands of times now, maybe more. I have received communion in stone churches in Vancouver, in Haiti's tent city churches, in an upper room across from the Vatican in Rome, in Calgary living rooms, in Texas megachurches, and in Regina leisure centers. I have crossed myself after partaking and I have also carried on in my day as if it matters nothing. I can repeat the words along with the preachers and barely internalize them.

But as I went forward on that evening, while the community

---

* Isaiah 2:4, 11:6, 35:1, and Revelation 21:4.

was singing, the woman who was offering bread and wine in my corner of the church quietly tucked the bread into my open palm and said to me, "This is the Body of Christ, given to you, Sarah." I closed my fingers around the hunk of bread and raised it toward the cup that was being held by her partner, who said, "This is the blood of Christ, poured out for you, Sarah." I dipped the bread into the wine and popped it into my mouth.

The bread, weighted with wine, sat on my tongue. I pressed it against the roof of my mouth and my knees buckled involuntarily. I quickly walked over to my chair in the front row and collapsed into it. I chewed and swallowed, suddenly aware of every taste, every reality of it, tears running down my face.

It felt like the line of time collapsed a bit, as if all that was and is and will be was present there. In that moment of tasting, something in my soul illuminated that I haven't been able to articulate even now, years later, about the welcome and faithfulness of Love for all of us hungry and thirsty ones.

SOME PART OF ME WOULD like to set up a banquet table in these woods, or maybe in my front yard, maybe on a street surrounded by public housing and safe-injection sites, it doesn't really matter. Maybe it would be a big farmhouse table knocked together by my carpenter husband; he'd love to do it, I know. I'd gather old metal lawn chairs and a tree stump, throw down picnic blankets and ratty old quilts. Less crackers and a quick sip of juice and more loaves of homemade bread and generous flasks of wine (and juice after all, to include sober folks like me, too). More people sitting around the table, reclining into each other, laughing and whispering good secrets. More toasts and tears, more bowls of grapes and chatter, more babies enjoying the sound of their own voices, more jars of honey and mugs of tea, more quilts on the grass, more of a family reunion.

I'd put stubs of candles into tin cans, string paper lanterns from the trees, trace a few prayer circles out of river stones, stuff wildflowers and dandelions into mason jars. Scatter buckets of sidewalk chalk for the kids. You can wear what you want, no robes required. Bring your friends, especially the rowdy ones Jesus would have sat right beside.

In fact, I'd stand in the field, in the streets, banging on pots and pans, maybe singing off-key, calling everyone out. It would be nice if you brought enough to share, or were at least willing to share your small bit, but you wouldn't have to. It seems to me that we feast best when we each bring something to the table.

By now I've learned that God is enough and no one else is in charge of the guest list, so I'm not worried. Doubters, dreamers, skeptics, people over it and done with it, prophets and policymakers, failures and influencers, come home. I'd like us all to sit down together, hands out to receive and also to give. Imagine if we were to pray, to talk, to sit in silence, to read Scripture, to speak over again the centuries of blessings, to go for a walk in the woods, maybe a swim, to laugh until our sides ache. I'd like to pour wine or grape juice into those never-used wedding crystal goblets we've been saving for a special occasion—let's blow the dust off of that stuff. If we're lucky, someone will drop one and there will be a glorious smashing.

We can feed each other with real food. We'll eat yeasty bread, tomatoes, strawberries, flatbread, curries, brisket, and bannock, until we are full. Receive it, celebrate it, take it, receive it, turn around and feed each other. Whatever lands in your lap, have a bite and keep passing, keep passing it along, we've got people to feed.

AND I WOULD TELL YOU that this—this feast, this food, the light in the trees, the wonder, these gorgeous flawed people, this gathering, this world—it's everything broken and made whole again. We are all remembering that, the best we can, most days, and Jesus is with us always, even to the end of the age. If I could, I'd say or sign your name and tell you, "This is the Body of Christ broken for you, this is the blood of Christ poured out for you." You always belonged at this rowdy table. And somewhere, nearby, over the hill, into yesterday and for tomorrow, someone would be singing, even as you walk away.

Alongside you,
S.

BENEDICTION

Dear Friend,

We've come to the end of our time together. Already I'm thinking of seven more things I'd like to tell you, but that's not how this works, we both know that by now. Now is the time for you to gather your things, bid your farewells, grab whatever will nourish you for the road ahead, and simply keep going with my blessing. I'm not under the illusion that what worked or works for me will always work for you, but it's been an honor to spend these pages with you, offering up the practices and learnings that have served me well out here in the wilderness.

I wrote a companion study guide for this book with a few practices and prayers, but I still want to end here the same way as always: with a benediction for you. You may not know how you feel about such things anymore, and the way that I pray may not be the way that you pray (or don't) anymore, but I hope you can receive this in the spirit with which I intend it—as a blessing to tuck into your pocket, wrap around your shoulders, lay your head upon at night when you sleep.

So here, take this with you for the journey along with my love and hope. Sometimes when we don't know what we think about anything, it's nice to just rest in someone else's faith for a while anyway, especially when we feel a bit out of sorts. Open your hands and receive whatever lands. Everywhere we are is already held in the love of God, even in those times when the night gathers and you are on your own.

FIRST, I PRAY FOR YOU to know, to believe, to make your home within the love of God. May you be stubbornly convinced of your own value and belovedness. May you know that you aren't a problem to be solved, you never were. Release the need for checklists and time lines; you're on a slower, more winding path that prioritizes wildflowers and cliffs, the salt tang of the sea and spruces. The wilderness is home to God, even the wilderness inside you.

As you wander through the wilderness, I pray for altars to surprise you, places where you encounter the wild goodness of the Spirit's comfort and the feathered strength of God's love. May you sense the shelter of that love, the gathering of that love, even when the path feels lonely at times. I pray that you would be surprised by streams in the desert, nourishing and clear-to-the-bottom water for your soul that reminds you over and over again of all the ways the sacred is still hiding in plain sight.

While your faith adapts in order to survive, I pray for you to find courage and companionship. I pray for generous gentleness around you, for you, and through you. I pray for your good heart, curious mind, and beloved body to know the gentleness of a good mother in Jesus. Receive the patience and kindness of the Spirit, offer it freely to everyone, including yourself. May that gentleness deliver you to an unforced rhythm of grace that reawakens you, recovers you, and restores you. May you receive losing your religion like the gift it will be to you in the end.

I know you're not alone, even when you feel profoundly lonely and abandoned. As my mother told me and I tell my children, people will talk and still your soul is fine. My mother would also want me to remind you that God's love is abundant life for you, beloved: not stingy, not mean, not harsh. May you know the love of God in your most bruised places as overflowing life and healing. May you dare to believe and set up camp in the life-giving abundance of that love.

I pray for an audacious hopefulness, one that takes suffering and loss as seriously as it takes faith and love. I know you won't glamorize hope, you understand the grit-in-your-teeth nature of hope too well for that. When you are most windblown and filthy, when you lift your head yet again, I pray for a smart-aleck smile to be on your lips. May you know the companionship and guidance of the stars and the Spirit as you keep going.

May all of the meaning you find and create bring you comfort and peace.

I pray for healing. I do. I do. We both know by now that healing doesn't come because we're so good at faking being fine. Tell the truth. And again, I pray for healing. I pray that every break and every wound would be met with restoration, grace, and meaning. May you learn to bless your losses, your discomfort, longings, and sorrow, too. Grieve what could have been and perhaps what should have been. Healing doesn't mean that pain disappears in a puff of smoke. I pray that you would embrace a plain, ordinary sort of healing that prioritizes rest, joy, goodness, ritual, compassion, and kindness. May you choose healing the way you're choosing courage: defiantly, lovingly, humbly.

May you become friends with your sorrow and longing. Honor with lament that engages God in your suffering. May the darkness and the slower path become friends to you. You don't keep time with anyone else but the Spirit now. Take all the time you need, you're not late or lagging.

May you evolve into someone who is more loving, who is healing, who is more acquainted with the fragility and beloved-ness of us all. Even as you name what you are Against, I pray that you would make room for the possibilities of what you are For in this world. Don't miss the invitation hiding there in your Against, something good is waiting on the other side. You might need time to live into it, it will be hard work, it will sometimes feel futile and small and ridiculous. And yet there you will be, with a dawning sense of what is possible and the guts to see it through.

I pray for you to have the courage to tell the truth, even to yourself and about yourself. I pray for a friend but also for good guides, therapists, teachers who will help you root out what is making you sick and equip you for the possibility of wholeness. May you learn to integrate your hope with your lament. May you learn to love your broken heart; each stitch of mending will be there on purpose. It will lead you home.

May you sense the hand of God beckoning in the invitation of your life. May you receive the sacred permission to say "I don't know" more often.

I pray for the boldness to repent and change direction. May your life change even as your mind and spirit change. May you move in the direction of your best hopes, turning toward what brings flourishing and healing to you and the world. I pray you will be met with forgiveness, but where that isn't possible, may you still find peace in repair and restoration.

I pray for a sacramental imagination that brazenly leans into hope. Keep company with God and learn a life of love. I pray for a homemade quilt, made up of the scraps from your grand-mothers and church mothers that you want to keep, everything worth keeping with you for the journey.

May you nurture your own belonging and build pockets of belonging for others. Not every place is for us, but when you know yours, I pray you would keep the door open and an eye out for the lonely ones who may wander by. May you expand your practices of belonging, finding community in the unex-pected places. Find good teachers again. I pray that your ability to discern would be sharpened, yes, and your critical thinking engaged right alongside your loving spirit. We're always invited to be in on what God is doing in the world; I pray you would find work that brings joy to you. May you find honor in what you put your time and energy toward. I pray for a peacemaker's posture in you, a disruptive and bold healing presence in this world.

And so I pray for joy. I pray for laughter and bright good-ness. I pray for inside jokes and glances that hold whole con-versations with kindred spirits. I pray for delight to be yours again, for the smallest of happiness to be an oasis. I pray that you would reclaim what brings you wonder and satisfaction, honor the food and the music, the people and the play that make you feel free.

AS WE SAY GOODBYE FOR now, I pray for the compass of Spirit to lead you forward. I hope our paths cross again. May you trust in the wilderness, knowing that, even now, you are held in the Love that holds everything.

Go with God.
With love,
S.
Ordinary Time, 2023

ACKNOWLEDGMENTS

Thank you to my friends and family, many of whom can bear witness to the fact that there isn't much tidiness or master planning in how I arrived at a lot of these ideas and practices. A particular thank-you to my Somewheres and my ASSS Sisters (don't worry, it's fine) as well as the fellow writers, artists, musicians, preachers, activists, and thinkers who continue to inspire, elevate, push, and challenge me. Thank you to my spiritual director, Tara Owens, and the team at Anam Cara. Thank you to the faith communities of my past and present, I remain (mostly) grateful.

Thank you to Evolving Faith, especially my friend and coconspirator, Ashleigh Nelson, and the entire team past and present, as well as all of our scattered community, for sharing your stories, your time, and your hearts with each other and me. I hold this as precious. Thank you to my friend Jeff Chu, I'm so grateful for our laughter, texts, and good work together through the years, but especially for the ways you've helped me to articulate and live into so many of these ideas. Beloved friend Rachel Held Evans, I miss you every single day, I will always hold you in my heart and my work with such love. Gratitude, love, and friendship always for Jim Chaffee, Amanda Held Opelt and her family, Peter and Robin Held, Dan and Jessie Evans and their little family.

Thank you to the Field Notes community and all of my readers over the years as I worked and wrote and wrestled with these practices in real time with you. Thank you for your support and companionship through the page and pixels, I never take this for granted.

Usually by the end of a manuscript, I have the realization that I wrote it for a particular person or persons, who are sort of standing in as icons for everyone else who will read it. And sure enough, about halfway through writing this book, I figured out I was writing it for the kids who used to gather in our living room back when we were youth pastors in the Texas Hill Country, for small groups, Bible studies, grilled cheese, and conversation. So to Bianca, Amber, Natalie, Keely, Abbie, and the dozens of other precious then-kids-now-grown-adults whose stories I'll never forget, you who sat on our battered green canvas couch all those years ago, this one ended up being for you. These are the things I would say if we were sitting in my living room all over again like we used to do. I'm so proud of you. You will always have me and Brian in your corner.

Thank you to my longtime literary agent and friend, Rachelle Gardner, for your tender heart, strong conviction, wise counsel, and steady presence. Thank you to the entire team at Convergent Books and Penguin Random House, especially my editors Becky Nesbitt and Derek Reed, along with everyone in production, marketing, publicity, sales, and design. I love working with you all, it's genuinely a joy.

Thank you to my sister and best friend, Amanda, and her family as well as my loving parents, David and Joan Styles. Thank you to my beloved children, Anne, Joseph, Evelynn, and Margaret: I love you, like you, adore you, delight in you as you were and you are and you will be, and I always will.

Thank you to my husband, Brian, for, well, everything. You're our sanctuary in this world. You make me so deeply happy. God, I love you.

And always, still, Jesus. God with us. I like being with You, out here, under the stars, where we can breathe a little in the companionable silence. You're even better than I could have imagined. It turned out, you were good news all along, trustworthy One.

NOTES

CHAPTER 1: WELCOME TO THE WILDERNESS

1. Rachel Held Evans, sermon at Evolving Faith Conference, October 26, 2018, audio recording available as part of *The Evolving Faith* (podcast), season 1, episode 1: "Evolution, Apocalypse, and Remembering Rachel Held Evans," https://evolvingfaith.com/podcast/season-1/blog-post-title-four-dac6d.

2. It feels weird to footnote my own book, but for the curious: Sarah Bessey, *Out of Sorts: Making Peace with an Evolving Faith* (New York: Howard Books, 2015), p. 88.

3. Lisa Sharon Harper, host, "The Roots of U.S. Exploitation of Immigrant Labor—Slavery and Peonage," *Freedom Road* (podcast), episode 18, July 3, 2019, transcript available at https://freedomroad.us/wp-content/uploads/2019/07/Freedom-Road-Podcast-Immigration-Exploitation-Labor-Episode-Transcript.pdf.

4. Christian Wiman, *My Bright Abyss: Meditation of a Modern Believer* (New York: Farrar, Straus and Giroux, 2013), p. 61.

CHAPTER 2: AN EVOLVING FAITH IS ANOTHER WAY THROUGH

1. Sarah Bessey, *Miracles and Other Reasonable Things: A Story of Unlearning and Relearning God* (New York: Howard Books, 2019), p. 5.

2. Richard Rohr, *Everything Belongs: The Gift of Contemplative Prayer* (Crossroad, 2003), pp. 112, 128.

3. Brian McLaren, *Faith After Doubt: Why Your Beliefs Stopped Working and What to Do About It* (New York: St. Martin's Essentials, 2021), appendix 1, "The Four Stages of Faith," p. 224.

4. Ibid., p. 182.

5. J.R.R. Tolkien, *The Fellowship of the Ring* (Boston: Houghton Mifflin, 1966), p. 278.

CHAPTER 3: MAKE YOUR PEACE WITH THIS TRUTH

1. Madeleine L'Engle, *A Swiftly Tilting Planet* (New York: Farrar, Straus and Giroux, 1978), p. 26.

2. Rohr, Fr. Richard. "Essential Teachings on Love: Selected." Modern Spiritual Masters Series. Introduction by Joelle Chase and Judy Traeger.

CHAPTER 4: DON'T BE AFRAID, YOU CAN'T WANDER AWAY FROM GOD'S LOVE

1. Rich Mullins, "Elijah," on *Rich Mullins* (Reunion Records, 1986).

2. K.J. Ramsey, *The Lord Is My Courage: Stepping Through the Shadows of Fear Toward the Voice of Love* (Grand Rapids, Mich.: Zondevan, 2022), p. 144.

3. Barbara Brown Taylor, sermon at Evolving Faith Conference, October 4, 2019, also on *The Evolving Faith* (podcast), season 2, episode 1, transcript available at https://evolvingfaith.com/podcast/season-2/episode-1.

4. Jonathan Edwards, "Sinners in the Hands of an Angry God: A Sermon" (Boston: S. Kneeland and T-Green, 1741), p. 15. Digital Commons access from University of Nebraska on October 2, 2023.

CHAPTER 5: CULTIVATE HOPE ON PURPOSE

1. Justo L. González, *Luke: Belief: A Theological Commentary on the Bible* (Louisville, Ky.: Presbyterian Publishing, 2010), p. 277.

2. Jason Upton, "Road to Emmaus" on *Dying Star* (Brentwood, Tenn.: Integrity Music), performed by and written by Jason Upton, 2002.

CHAPTER 6: TELL THE TRUTH AND LEARN TO LAMENT

1. Joan Didion, "On Keeping a Notebook," in *Slouching Towards Bethlehem* (New York: Farrar, Straus and Giroux, 1968; Picador Modern Classics), p. 204.

2. Originally identified in 1969 as the stages of dying in her book *On Death and Dying* (Macmillan). Later, she and her protegé David Kessler identified those same stages for grieving in their book *On Grief and Grieving: Finding the Meaning of Grief Through the Five Stages of Loss* (New York: Scribner, 2005).

3. Kübler-Ross and Kessler, *On Grief and Grieving,* Kindle, p. 7.

4. Glennon Doyle, *Untamed* (New York: Dial Press, 2020), p. 267.

5. Naomi Shihab Nye, "Kindness," in *Words Under the Words: Selected Poems* (Portland, Ore.: Eighth Mountain Press, 1995), p. 42.

6. Viktor E. Frankl, *Man's Search for Meaning* (United Kingdom: Rider, 1946).

7. David Kessler on Brené Brown's podcast, https://brenebrown.com /podcast/david-kessler-and-brene-on-grief-and-finding-meaning/, accessed December 27, 2022.

8. Amanda Held Opelt, *A Hole in the World: Finding Hope in Rituals of Grief and Healing* (Nashville, Tenn.: Worthy Publishing, 2022), pp. 10–11.

9. Ibid., p. 13.

10. John Selwood, "Principles of Inner Word: Psychological and Spiritual," *Journal of Transpersonal Psychology,* vol. 16, no. 1 (1984), p. 64.

11. Scott Berinato, "That Discomfort You're Feeling is Grief," *Harvard Business Review,* March 23, 2020. Accessed October 2, 2023.

12. Claus Westermann, *Praise and Lament in the Psalms* (Atlanta: John Knox Press, 1981), p. 152.

13. Soong-Chan Rah, *Prophetic Lament: A Call for Justice in Troubled Times* (Westmont, Ill.: InterVarsity Press, 2015), Kindle, p. 21.

CHAPTER 7: NOTICE YOUR OWN SACRAMENTAL LIFE

1. Rob Bell, *What We Talk About When We Talk About God* (New York: HarperOne, 2013), p. 76.

2. John O'Donohue, *Beauty: The Invisible Embrace* (New York: Harper-Collins, 2004), p. 17.

3. Luci Shaw, *Breath for the Bones: Art, Imagination and Spirit: A Reflection on Creativity and Faith* (Nashville: Thomas Nelson, 2009), p. 81.

4. Rachel Held Evans, *Evolving in Monkey Town: How a Girl Who Knew All the Answers Learned to Ask the Questions* (Grand Rapids, Mich.: Zondervan, 2010), p. 222. Now published as *Faith Unraveled: How a Girl Who Knew All the Answers Learned to Ask Questions.*

5. Zora Neale Hurston, *Their Eyes Were Watching God* (Champaign: University of Illinois Press, 1991), p. 27.

6. Katherine May, *Enchantment: Awakening Wonder in an Anxious Age* (New York: Riverhead Books, 2023), p. 8.

7. N. T. Wright, *Surprised by Hope: Rethinking Heaven, the Resurrection, and the Mission of the Church* (New York: HarperOne, 2008), p. 193.

CHAPTER 9: RECLAIM REPENTANCE

1. Chanequa Walker-Barnes, *I Bring the Voices of My People: A Womanist Vision for Racial Reconciliation* (Grand Rapids, Mich.: Eerdmans, 2019), p. 190. This line is in the context of her exploration of Alice Walker's *The Color Purple,* particularly Albert's repentance.

2. Brenda Salter McNeil, *Roadmap to Reconciliation: Moving Communities into Unity, Wholeness, and Justice* (Westmont, Ill.: InterVarsity Press, 2016), p. 22.

3. Book of Common Prayer, 1662.

4. Austin Channing Brown, *I'm Still Here: Black Dignity in a World Made for Whiteness* (New York: Convergent Books, 2018), p. 110. It's also important to name that this quote is in the context of white people confessing their racism to her, eager to unburden themselves and receive absolution from a Black woman. She writes, "White people really want this to be what reconciliation means: a Black person forgiving them for one racist sin. But just as I cannot make myself responsible for the transformation of white people, neither can I offer relief for their souls." A whole word in Chapter 7, "Nice White People."

CHAPTER 10: LEARN TO LOVE THE WORLD AGAIN

1. Maggie Smith, "First Fall," in *Good Bones* (North Adams, Mass.: Tupelo Press, 2017), p. 4.

2. K.J. Ramsey, *The Lord Is My Courage: Stepping Through the Shadows of Fear Toward the Voice of Love* (Grand Rapids, Mich.: Zondervan, 2022), p. 44.

3. Frederick Buechner, *Beyond Words: Daily Readings in the ABC's of Faith* (New York: HarperOne, 2009), Kindle, p. 138.

CHAPTER 11: NURTURE YOUR OWN BELONGING

1. Stanley Grenz, *Theology for the Community of God* (Grand Rapids, Mich.: Eerdmans, 1994), p. 464.

2. Ibid., p. 465.

3. "The Beloved Community, A Conversation Between bell hooks and George Brosi for Appalachian Heritage," available at https://doi.org /10.1353/aph.2012.0109.

4. Katherine May, *Enchantment: Awakening Wonder in an Anxious Age* (New York: Riverhead Books, 2023), pp. 97–98.

5. Diana Butler Bass, *Christianity After Religion: The End of Church and the Birth of a New Spiritual Awakening* (New York: HarperOne, 2013), p. 197.

6. Dr. Chanequa Walker-Barnes at Evolving Faith Conference, 2019, available at *Evolving Faith* (podcast), season 2, episode 2, https: //evolvingfaith.com/podcast/season-2/episode-2.

7. David P. Gushee, *After Evangelicalism: The Path to a New Christianity* (Louisville, Ky.: Westminster John Knox Press, 2019), p. 116.

8. Nedra Glover Tawwab, Instagram caption and post July 24, 2022, https://www.instagram.com/p/CgZngMigYFK/.

9. Brené Brown, *Daring Greatly: How the Courage to Be Vulnerable Transforms the Way We Live, Love, Parent, and Lead* (New York: Gotham Books, 2012), p. 171.

CHAPTER 12: LOOK FOR GOOD TEACHERS

1. Jen Hatmaker preached this message at Evolving Faith Conference, 2019; then she shared some snippets on Facebook, available at https://www.facebook.com/jenhatmaker/posts/2385914171507564.

2. Strong's Concordance 1381.

3. Kelley Nikondeha, *Defiant: What the Women of Exodus Teach Us About Freedom* (Grand Rapids, Mich.: Eerdmans, 2020), p. 75.

4. The final report of the Truth and Reconciliation Commission of Canada: volume 4 (2015) is available for download at the National Centre for Truth and Reconciliation, University of Manitoba web-

site, https://nctr.ca/records/reports/. It is also available in many public libraries in Canada.

5. Kaitlyn Curtice, *Native: Identity, Belonging, and Rediscovering God*
(Grand Rapids, Mich.: Brazos Press, 2020), p. 159.

6. Soong-Chan Rah, *The Next Evangelicalism: Freeing the Church from
Western Cultural Captivity* (Westmont, Ill.: InterVarsity Press, 2009),
p. 13.

CHAPTER 13: BECOME A NEW EXPLORER ON AN ANCIENT PATH

1. Natalie Kogan, "Five Life-Changing Lessons the KonMari Declut-
tering Method Taught Me," Happier website, https://www.happier
.com/blog/5-life-changing-lessons-the-konmari-decluttering-method
-taught-me/, n.d.

2. A. J. Swoboda, *After Doubt: How to Question Your Faith Without Losing It.* (Baker Publishing Group, 2021), p. 152.

3. Abraham Joshua Heschel, "On Prayer," in *Moral Grandeur and
Spiritual Audacity: Essays,* ed. Susannah Heschel (Farrar, Straus and
Giroux, 1996), p. 263.

CHAPTER 14: REMEMBER TO BE FOR, NOT JUST AGAINST

1. Liz Gilbert, April 12, 2016, Facebook post, https://www.facebook
.com/GilbertLiz/photos/a.356148997800555/1004594839622631
/?type=3.

2. Richard Cohen, *How to Write Like Tolstoy: A Journey into the Minds
of Our Greatest Writers* (New York: Random House, 2021), p. 145.

3. The monomyth of the hero's journey was explored by Joseph Campbell in his book *The Hero with a Thousand Faces* (Princeton, N.J.:
Princeton University Press, 1949). There are seventeen stages altogether.

4. According to my research, this phrase was first used by a Jesuit, Father Pedro Arrupe. Kira Dault, "What Is the Preferential Option for the Poor?" *U.S. Catholic* (January 22, 2015), https://uscatholic .org/articles/201501/what-is-the-preferential-option-for-the-poor /#:~:text=The%20phrase%20%E2%80%9Cpreferential%20option %20for,Catholic%20bishops%20of%20Latin%20America.

5. His Holiness the Dalai Lama and Archbishop Desmond Tutu, with Douglas Abrams, *The Book of Joy: Lasting Happiness in a Changing World* (Toronto: Penguin Canada, 2016), Kindle, p. 264.

6. This saying is usually attributed to Archbishop Desmond Tutu. For instance, in Bono, "A Clenched Fist and an Open Hand: Lessons Learned from Desmond Tutu" (*Time,* December 31, 2021), https: //time.com/6132224/desmond-tutu-bono/, accessed June 26, 2023.

CHAPTER 15: CHOOSE PEACEMAKING

1. Cole Arthur Riley, *This Here Flesh: Spirituality, Liberation, and the Stories That Make Us* (New York: Convergent Books, 2022), p. 97.

2. Walter Brueggemann, *Peace* (Des Peres, Mo.: Chalice Press, 2001), p. 15.

3. bell hooks, *Teaching Community: A Pedagogy of Hope* (Oxfordshire: Routledge, 2003), p. 197.

CHAPTER 16: YOU HAVE PERMISSION TO BE HAPPY

1. Parker J. Palmer, *Let Your Life Speak: Listening for the Voice of Vocation.* (Jossey-Bass, 1999).

2. Angela Williams Gorrell, *The Gravity of Joy: A Story of Being Lost and Found* (Grand Rapids, Mich.: Eerdmans, 2021), p. 173.

3. Kostadin Kushlev, "Is Happiness Selfish?" *Character and Context* (blog), Society for Personality and Social Psychology, https://spsp.org /news/character-and-context-blog/kushlev-selfish-happiness, published July 15, 2022, accessed March 15, 2023.

4. Brené Brown, *The Gifts of Imperfection: Let Go of Who You Think You're Supposed to Be and Embrace Who You Are* (Center City, Minn.: Hazelden, 2010), pp. 72–73.

5. David Steindl-Rast, *Gratefulness, the Heart of Prayer: An Approach to Life in Fullness* (Mahwah, N.J.: Paulist Press, 1984), p. 204.

6. Jason Isbell, "24 Frames," on *Something More Than Free* (Southeastern, 2015).

7. Jason Isbell, "Super 8," on *Southeastern* (Southeastern, 2013).

8. Susan Cain, *Bittersweet,* p. 72.

9. Kathy Escobar, *Practicing: Changing Yourself to Change the World* (Louisville, Ky.: Westminster John Knox Press, 2020), p. 202.

10. For the uninitiated, according to the Hideout Theatre, "Improvisation, or improv, is a form of live theatre in which the plot, characters and dialogue of a game, scene or story are made up in the moment. Often improvisers will take a suggestion from the audience, or draw on some other source of inspiration to get started." https://www.hideouttheatre.com/about/what-is-improv/, accessed June 3, 2023.

CHAPTER 17: NOW WE'RE JUST GETTING STARTED

1. Alla Katsnelson, "Stump-Grown Christmas Trees Are the Gift That Keeps on Giving," *Smithsonian* (December 20, 2018), https://www.smithsonianmag.com/science-nature/coppice-farming-grows-christmas-trees-keep-giving-180971068/, accessed again March 14, 2023.

ABOUT THE AUTHOR

SARAH BESSEY is the author or editor of five books, including the *New York Times* bestseller *A Rhythm of Prayer*. She also leads Evolving Faith, a conference and online community for people who are reimagining their faith with hope. Sarah lives in Calgary, Alberta, Canada, with her husband and their four children.